D1534769

America in an Arab Mirror

America in an Arab Mirror

Images of America in
Arabic Travel Literature,
1668 to 9/11 and Beyond

Edited by
Kamal Abdel-Malek and
Mouna El Kahla

AMERICA IN AN ARAB MIRROR
Copyright © Kamal Abdel-Malek and Mouna El Kahla, 2000.
All rights reserved.

First published as *America in An Arab Mirror: Images of America in Arabic Travel Literature: An Anthology* in hardcover in 2000 by St. Martin's Press LLC, 175 Fifth Avenue, New York, NY 10010. This revised edition, *America in An Arab Mirror: Images of America in Arabic Travel Literature, 1668 to 9/11 and Beyond* first published in paperback in 2011 by Palgrave Macmillan.

Where this book is distributed in the UK, Europe and the rest of the world, this is by Palgrave Macmillan, a division of Macmillan Publishers Limited, registered in England, company number 785998, of Houndmills, Basingstoke, Hampshire RG21 6XS.

Palgrave Macmillan is the global academic imprint of the above companies and has companies and representatives throughout the world.

Palgrave® and Macmillan® are registered trademarks in the United States, the United Kingdom, Europe and other countries.

ISBN: 978-0-230-62035-3

Library of Congress Cataloging-in-Publication Data is available from the Library of Congress.

A catalogue record of the book is available from the British Library.

Design by Letra Libre

First PALGRAVE MACMILLAN paperback edition: March 2011

10 9 8 7 6 5 4 3 2 1

Printed in the United States of America.

Transferred to Digital Printing in 2011

For A. Abdel-Malek,
my dear brother and my first Ustaadh, teacher,
who instilled in me the love of learning.

Semper fidelis.

Kamal Abdel-Malek

And to my kindhearted and supportive parents,
with my unbounded love:
I am now and will always be
proud to be your daughter.

Mouna El Kahla

Contents

IV
AMERICA IN THE EYES OF
ARAB WOMEN TRAVELERS

V
SATIRICAL VIEWS OF AMERICA

VI
COLONIAL SPANISH AMERICA IN THE EYES
OF A SEVENTEENTH-CENTURY ARAB (1668)

VII
EARLY EGYPTIAN TRAVELERS IN AMERICA:
MUHAMMAD ALI PASHA'S TRIP IN 1912

VIII
ACCOUNTS OF ARAB TRAVELERS
TO AMERICA BETWEEN 1996 AND 2000

IX
ACCOUNTS OF ARAB TRAVELERS
TO AMERICA AFTER 9/11

Preface

The first volume of this book appeared in 2000 and included the travel accounts of Arab visitors to America between 1895 and 1995. It was well received and proved to be of such importance that it was consulted and cited in the Congress Report on the 9/11 attacks.

This second volume covers the period between 1996 through 9/11, 2001, and beyond. It also fills in some gaps by inserting the following accounts:

1. The much earlier account of the first Arab voyager to Colonial Spanish America (Elias Al-Musili, 1668);
2. The account of the earliest Egyptian traveler to America (Muhammad Ali Pasha, 1912);
3. The travel account of the late Egyptian polymath Dr. Husayn Fawzi in his *Sinbad in the New World* (1984).

The new accounts in this volume are anthologized in a chronological order, not thematically as in the first volume. We deemed it too early to classify these accounts in a thematic arrangement. However, we can, at this stage, identify some prominent features of the accounts presented here:

1. Anti-American sentiments are much more pronounced but mixed with fascination of American lifestyles and popular culture.
2. In the views of the most recent Arab travelers, America is closely associated with Israel. There is hardly any account without references to the American-Israeli alliance; America's unqualified military, political, and financial support for Israel; America's double standard in dealing with Israel and the Arab world. America is slammed for its bias in favor of Israel and at times she and Israel are viewed as the common enemy of the Arab peoples. Some views express utter bafflement about America's insistence on allying itself with Israel even after thousands of American citizens were killed in the 9/11 attacks, attacks that are widely viewed as a result of American collusion with Israel.

3. America is projected as a female entity, seductive but deceptive at times. This is a carryover from the theme found in the previous volume of this anthology.

4. The noted presence in these recent accounts of Gulf Arab travelers to America: the Saudi Ghazi al-Qusaybi, Turki al-Dakhil, Nasir al-Din al-Zamil, and the Emirati Abd al-Aziz al-Musallam.

5. Accounts include more information about American history and politics than actual personal observations about American life. We come across references to the beginnings of the American history, Native Americans, the idea of frontiers, Manifest Destiny, American presidency, the American dream, and so on.

6. Only one additional travel writing from a female Arab author was identified to add to the others included in the first volume. She was the Egyptian, Wafaa Ibrahim, *One Hundred and Eighty Days in Yankeestan* (2002).

7. There are more fictional works with an American setting—we are referring here to both Sunallah Ibrahim's *Americanli* (2004) and Alaa al-Aswani's *Chicago* (2007).

8. Unexpectedly perhaps the American invasion and occupation of Iraq has provided a fertile context for satirical works: Yusuf Maati's, *Would You Like to Hate America?* (2003), and Yasir Qantush's parody, *The Egyptian Occupation of America* (2008). Much like the case in the first volume we notice that these satirical views of America are exclusive to Egyptian authors.

9. With this diverse body of Arab travelogues about America, can we really talk about an Arab Occidentalism, a systematic literature of cultural stereotyping? Is this a counter-Orientalism, an Arab response to centuries of Western stereotypical writings about them? An Arab way of saying: we too can subjugate you, Westerners, to our tourist, voyeuristic gaze; we too can produce a discourse that describes, analyzes, categorizes, stereotypes, and even satirizes your manners, customs, and outlooks on life?

In this second volume we have provided for the first time, in any language, an anthology on the major travel accounts of Arab visitors to America from the seventeenth century to the present. We present these selections to Western readership, especially the Americans among them, with the hope that by so doing we shed light on little known aspects of Arab-American relations. We plan to produce in the near future a detailed study of these Arab views of America in order that we may further the discussion on this important topic.

For her thorough reading, editorial comments on earlier drafts of this book, and her assistance and support, we would like to express our gratitude to Jennifer Sheldon.

Kamal Abdel-Malek and Mouna El Kahla
Dubai, UAE, December 2010

List of Accounts of Arab Travelers
to America According to Their
Date of Publication (1668–2008)

1668

Musili, Elias al-. *Al-Dhahab wa al-Asifa; Rihlat Elias al-Musili ila Amrika: Auwal Rihla Arabiyya ila al-Alam al-Jadid* (The Gold and the Tempest: The Journey of Elias al-Musili to America, The First Arab Journey to the New World). Ed. Nuri al-Jarrah. Abu Dhabi: Dar al-Suwaydi; Beirut: Al-Muassasa al-Arabiyya, 2001.

———. *An Arab's Journey to Colonial Spanish America: The Travels of Elias al-Musili in the Seventeenth Century.* Translated from the Arabic and edited by Caesar E. Farah. Syracuse University Press, 2003.

1895

Rustum, Mikhail Asad. *Kitab al-Gharib fi al-Gharb* (A Stranger in the West: Trip of Mikhail Asad Rustum to America, 1885–1894) 2d ed. Beirut: Dar al-Hamra, 1992.

1912

Ali Pasha, Al-Amir Muhammad. *Al-Rihla al-Amrikiyya, 1912* (A Passage to America, 1912). Ed. Ali Ahmad Kan'an. Abu Dhabi: Dar al-Suwaydi; Beirut: Al-Muassasa al-Arabiyya [2004],

1924

Hitti, Philip. *Amrika fi Nazar Sharqi aw Thamani Sanawat fi al-Wilayat al-Muttahida al-Amrikiyya* (America in the Eyes of an Easterner, Or Eight Years in the United States). Cairo: Dar al-Hilal, 1924.

1930

Batanuni, Muhammad Labib, al-. *Al-Rihla ila Amrika* (The Trip to America). Cairo: Maktabat al-Khanji, 1930.

1946?

Taymur, Mahmud. *Abu al-Hawl Yatir* (The Flying Sphinx [in America]). Cairo: Beirut: al-Maktaba al-Asriyya, n.d.

1951
Qutb, Sayyid. "Amrika allati Raayt" (The America I Have Seen). *Al-Risala,*
    vol. 2, no. 957 (5 November, 1951), pp. 1245–1247; no. 959 (19 Novem-
    ber, 1951), pp. 1301–1306; no. 961 (3 December, 1951), pp. 1357–1360.

1954
Khalid, Zaki. *Amrika That al-Mikroskob* (America under the Microscope).
    Cairo: Maktabat al-Nahda al-Misriyya, 1954.

1955
Mahmud, Zaki Najib. *Ayyam fi Amrika* (My Days in America). Cairo: Mat-
    baat Lajnat al-Talif wa al-Tarjama wa al-Nashr, 1955.

1962
Jabri, Shafiq. *Ard al-Sihr* (The Land of Magic). Damascus: al-Fann al-Ha-
    dith al-Alami, 1962.

1962?
Sidqi, Jadhibiyya. *Amrika wa Ana* (America and I). Cairo: Maktabat al-
    Nahda al-Misriyya, n.d.

1972
Awad, Mahmud. *Siyaha Gharamiyya* (A Love Tour). Cairo: Muassasat
    Akhbar al-Yawm, 1972.

1979
Mustafa, Ahmad. *Muhajir ila Amrika* (An American Immigrant). Cairo: Dar
    al-Maarif, 1979.

1980?
Idris, Yusuf. *Niyu Yurk Thamanin* (New York 80). Cairo: Maktabat Misr, n.d.

1982
Hammuda, Adil. *Amrika, al-Janna wa al-Nar* (America: Paradise and Hell-
    fire). Cairo: Mussasat Ruz al-Yusuf, 1982.

1983
Kamal, Karima. *Bint Misriyya fi Amrika* (An Egyptian Girl in America).
    Cairo: Maktabat Gharib, 1983.

1984
Fawzi, Husayn. *Sinbad in the New World* (Sindbad ila al-Alam al-Jadid).
    Cairo: Dar al-Maarif, 1984.

1986
al-Hasan, Yusuf. *Min Awraq Washington* (The Washington Memoirs). Cairo:
    Dar al-Mustaqbal al-Arabi, 1986.

1987

Ashur, Radwa. *Al-Rihla: Ayyam Taliba Misriyya fi Amrika* (The Trip: The Days of an Egyptian Female Student in America). Cairo: Maktabat Madbuli, 1987.

1987

Haridi, Ahmad. *Amrika Sirri Jiddan* (America [Top Secret]). Cairo: Maktabat Madbuli, 1987.

1988

Sharabi, Hisham. *Al-Jamr wa al-Ramad: Dhikrayat Muthaqqaf Arabi* (Embers and Ashes: Memoirs of an Arab Intellectual). 2d ed. Beirut: Dar al-Talia, 1988.

1989

Hasan al-Alfi, Muhammad. *Amrika: al-Jinz wa al-Skkin* (America: The Jeans and the Switchblade). Cairo: Mahmud al-Jiddawi, 1989.

Amin, Mustafa. *Amrika al-Dahika Zaman: Mudhakkirat Talib Muflis fi al-Wilayat al*-Muttahida (Cheerful America of the Past: Journal of A Penniless Student in the United States). Cairo: Muassast Akhbar al-Yawm, 1989.

1990 al-Sadani, Mahmud. *Amrika Ya Wika* (America, You Cheeky Devil). Cairo: Dar al-Hilal, 1990.

1991

Imara, Mahmud. *Amrika li al-Bay* (America for Sale). Cairo: Matabi al-Ahram, 1991.

Abu Zayd, Layla. *Amrika: al-Wajh al-Akhar* (America's Other Face). Casablanca: Matbaat al-Najah al-Jadida, 1991.

1993

Salem, Ali. *Hikayati maa Iva* (My Story with Eva [Ivana Trump]. Cairo: Maktabat Madbuli al-Saghir, 1993.

1995

Sarhan, Hala. *Amrika Khabt Laz* (America . . . The Way It Is). Cairo: Dar al-Shuruq, 1995.

1996

Hadidi Hisham al-. *New York Awwal Marra* (The First Glimpse of New York). Cairo: Al-Dar al-Misriyya al-Lubnaniyya, 1996.

1998

Sarkis, Adil Ahmad. *Rihlat Misri fi Amrika* (An Egyptian in America). Cairo: Madbuli, 1998

From 9/11 and Beyond:

2001

Jamal, Samir al-. *Wahid Amrikri bi-Mayonnaise* (One Americano with Mayonnaise, Please). Cairo: Jazirat al-Ward, 2001.

2002

Ibrahim, Wafaa. *Ma'ah wa-Thamanun Yawman fi Bilad al-Yankee* (One Hundred and Eighty Days in Yankeestan). Cairo: Dar Gharib, 2002.

Qusaybi, Ghazi Abd al-Rahman al-. *Al-Awda ila CaliforniaSa'ihan* (Returning to California as a Tourist) 4h ed. Beirut: Dar al-Saqi, 2002.

2003

Hilal, Rida. *Tafkik Amrika: Ma-ba'd Ahdath 11 Simbtambir* (Deconstructing America: 9/11 and Its Aftermath) 3d ed. Cairo: Dar Misr al-Mahrusa, 2003.

2003

Jawwadi, Muhamad al-. *Shams al-Asil fi Amrika.* (Dusk in America) 3d ed. Cairo: Dar Jihad, 2003.

Maati, Yusuf. *Tihibb Tikrah Amrika?* (Would You Like to Hate America?). Cairo: Atlas, 2003.

2004

Musallam, Abd al-Aziz al-. *Mada'in al-Rih* (Cities of Wind). Abu Dhabi: Dar al-Suwaydi li al-Nashr, 2004.

Ibrahim, Sunallah. *Amrikanli (Amri Kana Li)* (Americanli) 2d ed. Cairo: Dar al-Mustaqbal al-Arabi, 2004.

Zamil, Nasir al-Din Muhammad al-. *Limadha Yakrahunana?* (Why Do They Hate Us?). Riyadh: Maktabat al-Ubaykan, 2004.

2005

Abd al-Hakim, Mansur. *Al-Imbraturiyya al-Amrikiyya, al-Bidaya wa al-Nihaya* (The Rise and Fall of the American Empire). Damascus and Cairo: Dar al-Kitab al-Arabi, 2005.

2006

Zuhayr Wasini, *Fi Ahdan Condaleeza Rice wa-Bidun Khasa'ir* (Embrace Condaleeza Rice at Your Own Risk). Tangiers: Ifzarn li al-Tibaa wa al-Nashr, 2006.

2007

Aswani, Alaa al-. *Chicago.* Cairo: Dar al-Shuruq, 2007.

Al-Dakhil, Turki. *Sa'udiyyun fi Amrika* (Saudis in America) 2d ed. Riyadh: Ubaykan, 2007.

I

America in the Eyes of a Nineteenth-Century Arab

A Stranger in the West:
The Trip of Mikhail Asad Rustum to America,
1885–1894

MIKHAIL ASAD RUSTUM was born in Lebanon in the mid-nineteenth
century and emigrated to the United States in the 1880s where he
settled in Philadelphia. He published his *A Stranger in the West: The Trip
of Mikhail Asad Rustum to America, 1885–1894,* in New York in 1895.
His is probably the first account, or one of the first accounts, of an
Arab traveler in the United States.

The Contrast Between American Western Ways and [Middle] Eastern Ways and the Differences Even in Climate and Natural Phenomena

1. We are [Middle] Easterners	1. They are American Westerners
2. When it is daylight in our country	2. It is nighttime in theirs
3. Our word for "sun" is feminine;	3. The opposite the "moon" is masculine
4. We write from right to left	4. They write from left to right
5. We say literally: "a book good" (putting the attribute after its noun)	5. They say "a good book" (using the opposite order)
6. We say: "approx. seven eight days"	6. They say: "approx. eight seven days"
7. Our men walk ahead of our women	7. Their women walk ahead of their men
8. We say: "What would you like to eat today, sir?"	8. They ask: "What would you like to eat today, ma'am?"
9. Women submit to their men	9. Men submit to their ladies

10. The young man proposes to his bride-to-be

10. The young woman proposes to her husband-to-be

11. All life long, children submit to their parents

11. Only until they reach 21

12. Our clothes are loose and comfortable

12. Theirs are tight and uncomfortable

13. Our women don't always follow every fashion

13. Theirs follow a new fashion every day

14. We take off our shoes when we enter homes

14. They take off only their hats

15. We visit one another during holidays and celebrations

15. They don't allow any visit

16. We are always ready to receive guests who drop in on us

16. They refuse to receive guests who arrive unannounced

17. We say: "Please come over to our home we want to see you"

17. They say: "Please come over to our home to see us"

18. Our bread is usually flat and thin

18. Theirs is thick

19. We eat fresh meat

19. They eat their meat at least one week old, if not older

20. We eat our fruit after the meal

20. They eat theirs before the meal

21. We sprinkle salt on tomatoes

21. On tomatoes they sprinkle sugar instead; as for the salt, they actually sprinkle it on watermelon!

22. What we weigh

22. They measure, and vice-versa

23. We rejoice over the birth of a baby boy

23. They rejoice over the birth of a baby girl

24. We use cloth diapers for infants.

24. Their infants go without cloth diapers. When their girls reach puberty they have the freedom to wear corsets

Songs of the Americans with a Translation into Arabic

[The songs are cited in the English original followed by Arabic transliteration as well as translation.—Editor]

I

There is a flower within my heart
Daisy, Daisy

Planted by one of your startling darts
Planted by Daisy Belle
And whether she loves me or not, I can't tell
Daisy, Daisy Belle
Daisy, Daisy, give me your answer though I am half crazy
All for the love of you
It won't be styling marriage
We can't afford a carriage
But you look sweet about the seat
Of a bicycle built for two
                              II
Two little girls blue dress
Two little girls blue
We were brothers, were sisters
And learn to love too
One little girl in blue dress
Won your father's heart
Became your mother, I married the other
And we have worked about

The man who put this song to music is said to have earned $15,000. The lyric writer who composed the following song is said to have earned $50,000:

Sweet Mary come to me
Come to me sweet Mary
Not because your face is for love to see

The following song is sung to a tune similar to one of our own [Arabic] songs:

I have Car in Baltimore Street
Car runs from her front door
She lives in the third floor
Bum tarara bountry boo tarara bountry

Our song runs:

Yammu l-fustaan il-biyhill
Wadda'naaki bidnaa nifill
[O lady with a bright dress
It is time to say goodbye to you and depart]

—Translated by Kamal Abdel-Malek

II

The Making of an Image:
America as the Unchanged Other,
America as the Seductive Female

2.

"The America I Have Seen":
In the Scale of Human Values (1951)

SAYYID QUTB was Egypt's most prominent Islamic activist and the most famous member of the Muslim Brothers organization until his execution by Nasser's regime in 1966. One of his biographers compares his overall standing as an Islamic thinker and activist to that of Ayatollah Khomeini. He is the author of several works on Islamist ideology including his radical *Milestones* (1964) for the publication of which he was hanged. In 1948, he was sent by the Egyptian Ministry of Education to the United States to study American pedagogical methods. He studied at Wilson's Teachers' College (now the University of the District of Columbia); the University of Northern Colorado's Teachers' College, where he earned an M.A. in education, and at Stanford University. Upon his return to Egypt in 1950, he published an account of his stay in the United States in the Egyptian magazine *Al-Risala* under the title, "The America I Have Seen." The same account was later included in a book edited by Abd al-Fattah al-Khalidi under the telling title, *Amrika min al-Dakhil bi-Minzar Sayyid Qutb* (America from the Inside through the Eyes of Sayyid Qutb). The title page has a drawing of the American flag shown partly folded with a blood-stained, black-striped flag beneath it. America may appear to be one thing, but inside it is something else totally.

First Episode

America: Location and Privilege

America, the New World, is that vast, far-flung world that occupies in the mind's eye more space than it really does on this earth. Imaginations and dreams glimmer on this world with illusion and wonder. The hearts of men fall upon it from every valley, men from every race and color, every walk of life, and every sect and creed.

America, the vast expanses of land that stretch from the Atlantic to the Pacific. America is the inexhaustible material resources, strength and manpower. It is the huge factories, unequaled in all of civilization. It is the awesome, incalculable yields, the ubiquitous institutes, laboratories, and museums. American genius in management and organization evokes wonder and admiration. America's bounty and prosperity evokes the dreams of the Promised Land. The beauty that is manifested in its landscape, in the faces and physiques of its people is spellbinding. America conjures up pleasures that acknowledge no limit or moral restraint, dreams that are capable of taking corporeal shape in the realm of time and space.

America's Share of Human Values

This great America: What is its worth in the scale of human values? And what does it add to the moral account of humanity? And, by the journey's end, what will its contribution be?

I fear that a balance may not exist between America's material greatness and the quality of its people. And I fear that the wheel of life will have turned and the book of time will have closed and America will have added nothing, or next to nothing, to the account of morals that distinguishes man from object, and indeed, mankind from animals.

The Measure of Civilization

The true value of every civilization that man has known lies not in the tools man has invented or in how much power he wields. Nor does it lie in the yields his hands have harvested. Most of the value of civilizations lay in what universal truths and worldviews they have attained. These achievements elevate feelings, edify consciences, and add depth to man's perception of the values of all life, and human life in particular. They increase the distance between man and animal in feelings and behavior, through man's estimation of life and things.

As for the invention of tools, the wielding of powers, or the making of objects, these things are in and of themselves weightless in the scale of human values. They serve merely as indicators of another fundamental value, that is the extent to which the human element of man is elevated, how far his steps have taken him from the world of things and the world of animals, and what has been added to his human account of wealth and reflections on life.

So, in his feelings for this life, this fundamental value is the place of comparison and balance between one civilization and another, and one philosophy and another. Moreover, it is the lasting account and is relevant to future civilizations whereas tools break down and objects perish, only to be replaced by newer tools and objects from one moment to another anywhere on this earth.

The Field of American Innovation

It appears that all American ingenuity is concentrated in the field of work and production, so much so that no ability remains to advance in the field of human values. America's productivity is unmatched by any other nation. It has miraculously elevated life to levels that cannot be believed. But man cannot maintain his balance before the machine and risks becoming a machine himself. He is unable to shoulder the burden of exhausting work and forge ahead on the path of humanity, he unleashes the animal within.

America: The Peak of Advancement and the Depth of Primitiveness

The researcher of American life will stand at first puzzled before a wondrous phenomenon, a phenomenon that exists nowhere else on earth. It is the case of a people who have reached the peak of growth and elevation in the world of science and productivity, while remaining abysmally primitive in the world of the senses, feelings, and behavior. A people who has not exceeded the most primordial levels of existence, and indeed, remain far below them in certain areas of feelings and behavior. But the confusion vanishes after scruitinizing the past and present of this people, and the reason that this zenith of civilization has combined with this nadir of primitiveness is revealed.

The Balanced Composition of Man

In the ancient world, man first believed in the unknown power of nature and around it wove myths and legends. Then, he believed in religion, and his soul was flooded with its lights and revelations. Then, he believed in art, and his yearnings materialized as colors, tunes, and rhythms. And finally, after his self had been torn between a myriad of faiths, colors of feelings, differing manifestations of life's images, and the exaggerations of imagination, he believed in science. This belief in science took place only after his soul had been tamed by religion, his senses edified by art, and his behavior pruned by convocation, and after his values and principles had been shaped by the reality of history and his free yearnings. And while these principles and values may or may not have been fulfilled in daily life, at least they found echoes in the conscience and in feelings. There was hope of fulfillment because the mere presence of these principles and values in the abstract world was a great step for mankind on the path to humanity, and a luminous beam of hope for their eventual realization in daily life.

The Deformed Birth of the American Man

In America, man was born with science, and thus believed in it alone. In fact, he only believed in one kind of science, and that was applied science. Since he received nature as an untamed, stubborn virgin, and fought to build his homeland with his bare hands, applied science was his greatest ally in his violent struggle. Applied science reached out to him with effective tools for creating, building, organizing, and producing.

America as a Virgin Land

The American has not yet finished with the building stage, for there remains interminable, incalculable expanses of virgin land, untouched by any hand, and virgin forests untrodden by any foot, and mines that have neither been excavated nor depleted. There remains for the American the continuation of his first construction effort, in spite of his having achieved the peak of organization and production.

The Psychological State of the First Americans

And we would do well not to forget the psychological state that wave after wave, and generation after generation of Americans brought to this land. For they brought a blend of discontent with the life of the Old World and the desire for freedom from its rigid traditions whether they were onerous, corrupt traditions or sound and necessary ones. This psychological state springs from an enduring desire for wealth by any means, and for the possession of the largest possible share of pleasures and compensation for the effort expended to acquire wealth.

The Origin of the Americans

And we would do well also not to forget the social and mental state of the majority of these first waves of immigrants who formed the seeds of this new nation. For these waves were composed of groups of adventurers, and groups of criminals. The adventurers came seeking wealth, pleasure, and adventure, while the criminals were brought to this land from the lands of the British Empire as labor for construction and production.

Applied Science and Human Values

These combinations of entanglements, and of waves of people naturally encouraged and fostered primitive characteristics in this new nation, and ignored and resisted the elevated characteristics of some of the nation's individuals and groups. So the primal urges were revitalized, as if man retraced his first steps, with one difference, in the case of America, primitive man is armed with science, with which he was born, and which guided his steps. And science in itself, and especially applied science, plays no role in the field of human values, or in the world of the soul and feelings. And this narrowed his horizons, shrank his soul, limited his feelings, and decreased his place at the global feast, which is so full of patterns and colors.

The Struggle of the First American with Nature

And one may be amazed when reading the stories of the first pilgrims to America in its early days, and imagine their epic, amazing struggles against a defiant nature in far-flung, desolate lands, and even before this, braving the ocean's horrific squalls and its conquering waves, in their small, fragile vessels. As soon as these pilgrims landed upon the rocks, with their vessels destroyed or damaged, they faced the uncharted forests, the tortuous mountain mazes, the fields of ice, the thundering hurricanes, and the beasts, serpents, and vermin of the forest. One may be amazed at how all this did not leave a shadow upon the American spirit and inspire a belief in the majesty of nature and that which is beyond nature, opening for the American spirit a window on things that are more than matter and the world of matter.

The Secret of the Deformed American Character

However, this amazement vanishes when one remembers that mixture of the early American pilgrims and their surrounding conditions. They tackled nature with the weapons of science and the strength of the muscle, so nothing existed within them besides the crude power of the mind and the overwhelming lust for the sensual pleasure. No windows to the world of the spirit or the heart or tender sentiment were opened to the Americans as they were opened to the first humans. A great deal of this world of spirit, heart, and tender sentiment was preserved by the first humans, and much of this continued to be preserved even in the age of science, and added to the account of human values that endured through time.

And when humanity closes the windows to faith in religion, faith in art, and faith in spiritual values altogether, there remains no outlet for its energy to be expended except in the realm of applied science and labor, or to be dissipated in sensual pleasure. And this is where America has ended up after four hundred years.

Second Episode

The American Primitiveness

Despite his advanced knowledge and superlative work, the American appears to be so primitive in his outlook on life and its humanitarian aspects that it is puzzling to the observer. This clear contradiction may make the Americans appear as an eccentric nation in the eyes of foreigners who observe the life of this nation from afar and are at a loss to reconcile such an industrial civilization, with its precise order and organization of labor, with such primitiveness of feeling and manner, a primitiveness that reminds one of the days when man lived in jungles and caves!

Primitiveness in Athletics

It seems the American is primitive in his appreciation of muscular strength and the strength of matter in general. To the extent that he overlooks principles, values, and manners in his personal life, in his family life, and in his social life, except in the realm of work, and economic and monetary relationships. This primitiveness can be seen in the spectacle of the fans as they follow a game of football, played in the rough American style, which has nothing to do with its name (football), for the foot does not take part in the game. Instead, each player attempts to catch the ball with his hands and run with it toward the goal, while the players of the opposing team attempt to tackle him by any means necessary, whether this be a blow to his stomach, or crushing his arms and legs with great violence and ferocity. The sight of the fans as they follow this game, or watch boxing matches or bloody, monstrous wrestling matches . . . is one of animal excitement born of their love for hardcore violence. Their lack of attention to the rules and sportsmanship to the extent that they are enthralled with the flowing blood and crushed limbs, crying loudly, everyone cheering for his team. Destroy his head. Crush his ribs. Beat him to a pulp. This spectacle leaves no room for doubt as to the primitiveness of the feelings of those who are enamored with muscular strength and desire it.

American Love for Peace An Illusion

And with this primitive spirit the American people follow the struggles of groups and parties, and the struggles of nations and peoples. I cannot fathom how this strange illusion that Americans love peace took root in the world, especially in the East.

The American and the Hunger for War

Indeed, the American is by his very nature a warrior who loves combat. The idea of combat and war runs strong in his blood. It is evident in his manner and this is what agrees with his history. For the first waves of people left their homelands, heading for America with the intention of building and competing and struggling. And once there, some of them killed others, as they were composed of groups and factions. Then they all fought against the original inhabitants of the land (the red Indians), and they continue to wage a bloody war against them until this very moment. Then the Anglo-Saxons killed the Latinos and pushed them south toward central and southern America. Then these Americanized people turned against their mother country, England, in a destructive war led by George Washington until they obtained their independence from the British crown.

The True Motivations for the Manumission of American Slaves

Then the North fought the South under the command of Abraham Lincoln in a war that was called "the freeing of the slaves." But its true motivation was economic competition. The slaves that had been captured from central Africa to work in the land were fragile and could not withstand the cold climate of the North, so they were moved to the South. The result was that the builders of the South found cheap labor that was unavailable in the North. So they achieved economic superiority. For this reason, the Northerners declared war for the manumission of the slaves!

America Emerges from Isolation

The period of isolation passed, and its politics ended, when America entered the First World War. Then it entered the Second World War. Now it is starting a war in Korea, and a third world war is not far behind! I really cannot understand how this illusion came into being, given this nation's history with warfare.

The American View of Death

Physical vitality is sacred to the American, and weakness, no matter what its cause, is a crime: a crime that cannot be atoned for in any way, a crime that remains undeserving of compassion or care. The matter of morals and rights are an illusion in the conscience of the American, he cannot taste it. Be strong, and you will have everything. Or be weak and no ideology can help you, and there will be no place for you in the great realm of living. As for him who dies, he has committed, naturally, the crime of death. He loses all his rights to care and respect! Did he not die?

Americans Joke About the Injured

I was at George Washington Hospital in the capital city, and it was evening. Suddenly there was some commotion of unknown origin that drew much attention. And the patients who were able to move began leaving their beds and their rooms and coming into the hallway to take a closer look. Then they began to gather together inquiring about the source of this spectacle in the hospital's usually quiet life. We learned after a while that one of the hospital's employees was injured in an elevator accident and was in critical condition, indeed, he was in the final round of death. One of the American patients went to see for himself, and returned to tell those gathered in the hallway what he had seen. When the ghost of death lingers in a place, there is no greater reverence to it, nor more solemnity than in a hospital. But here was this American who began laughing and chuckling while he mimicked the appearance of the injured, dying man, and the way his neck was struck by the elevator, his head crushed, and his tongue dangled from his mouth on the side of his face! And I waited to see signs of disgust or disapproval from those listening, but the vast majority of them began laughing joyously at this odious act.

Laughing beside the Corpse of a Loved One

For this reason I am not surprised when some of my friends relate what they see and hear about death and its impact on the American consciousness.

A friend once told me that he was attending a funeral when the body of the head of the household was presented in a glass coffin—according to American custom—so that the friends of the deceased could pass by his body to bid him the final farewell and gaze upon him for the last time, one after another in a long line. When the procession ended, they all gathered in the reception room. What struck him was that there was no respect as they began mocking and making jokes about the deceased and other individuals. His wife and family took part in this, giving rise to joyful laughter in the cold silence of death, around the body that was shrouded in burial cloths.

An American Woman Carouses while Her Husband's Corpse Lies at Home

The Director of the Egyptian State scholarships in Washington was invited to a party with his wife. Before the engagement, his wife fell ill, so he called up to apologize for not being able to attend because of this emergency. But the hosts replied that there was no need to apologize as he could attend the party alone, which would actually be a good stroke of luck, since one of the women invited to the party had lost her husband suddenly before the party. She thus would have been alone there, so it was her good fortune that she could now have a companion!

An American Woman Speaks of Her Recently Deceased Husband

I once entered the house of an American woman who was helping me with my English during the first period of my stay in America. So I found there one of her female friends, and they were having a conversation that I caught the end of. This friend said, "I was lucky because I had taken out insurance on his life. Even his treatment cost very little because I had insured him with the Blue Cross," and she smiled.

Then she excused herself and left. I remained with the woman of the house and I assumed that her friend had been talking about her dog, and I was amazed that she did not exhibit any signs of distress at his death! But no sooner had I observed this than she said, without my asking, "She was speaking of her husband. He died three days ago."

And it appeared to her that I was stunned that her friend could speak this matter-of-factly about her husband merely three days after his death. Her seemingly sound and convincing excuse was, "He was ill! He had fallen sick more than three months before his death!"

The Funeral of the Birds in Egypt

My memory took me back to a scene that had a very profound emotional effect on me. Indeed, the effects have lasted on my mind for many years. I had in mind to write down this thought under the title, "The Funeral of the Birds." This was a scene of a group of chickens we raised in our home. The chickens gathered silently, spellbound and shocked around a chicken that had been slaughtered. It was an emotional surprise for everyone who had been in the house. A surprise unexpected from birds as low on the evolutionary scale as these chickens. Indeed, the shock was so great that we did not dare slaughter another chicken within the sight of this group of birds!

The Sadness of the Ravens over Their Dead

And the sight of the ravens when one of their own dies is a sight that many are accustomed to seeing. It is a sight that is hard to describe without mentioning that these birds must know "sadness," "emotion," and "kinship"! For a group of ravens will hover in circles, shrieking and wailing, until they carry the body of the deceased one and fly away. All this points to the gravity of death in the world of birds!

The Drought in American Life

The sanctity of death may be a natural instinct. So it is not the primitiveness of feeling that has erased the sanctity of death in the American soul. Rather, it is the drought of sentimental sympathy in their lives, and the foundation of their lives upon monetary and material measures, and sheer physical gratification. Americans intentionally deride what people in the Old World hold sacred, and their desire is to contrast themselves with the customary ways of the people there. Otherwise, the Americans would say, what merit does the New World have over the Old World?

The Feelings of Americans toward Religion Are Primitive

And what is said about their feelings toward death may also be said about their feelings toward religion.

Churches without Life

There is no people who enjoys building churches more than the Americans. To the extent that I once stayed in a town with no more than ten thousand inhabitants, yet within it I found over twenty churches! And most of them do not go to church on Sunday mornings and evenings, but instead on general holidays and holidays for local saints, who far outnumber the "saints" of the common Muslims in Egypt. All this notwithstanding there is no one further than the American from appreciating the spirituality of religion and respect for its sacraments, and there is nothing farther from religion than the American's thinking and his feelings and manners.

Churches for Carousal and Enjoyment

If the church is a place for worship in the entire Christian world, in America it is for everything but worship. You will find it difficult to differentiate between it and any other place. They go to church for carousal and enjoyment, or, as they call it in their language "fun." Most who go there do so out of necessary social tradition, and it is a place for meeting and friendship, and to spend a nice time. This is not only the feeling of the people, but it is also the feeling of the men of the church and its ministers.

The Clubs of the Church and Their Attractions

In most churches there are clubs that join the two sexes, and every minister attempts to attract to his church as many people as possible, especially since there is a tremendous competition between churches of different denominations. And for this reason, each church races to advertise itself with lit, colored signs on the doors and walls to attract attention, and by presenting delightful programs to attract the people much in the same way as merchants or showmen or actors. And there is no compunction about using the most beautiful and graceful girls of the town, and engaging them in song and dance, and advertising.

A Church's Party Program

This is an example of the text of an advertisement for a church party that was posted in the student's union of one of the colleges.

Sunday, October 1st, 6:00 P.M., snacks, magic games, puzzles, contests, fun

There is nothing strange in this, for the minister does not feel that his job is any different from that of a theater manager, or that of a merchant. Success comes first and before everything, and the means are not important, and this success will reflect on him with fine results: money and stature. The more people that join his church, the greater is his income. Likewise, his respect and recognition is elevated in the community, because the American by his nature is taken with grandeur in size and numbers. It is his first measure of the way he feels and evaluates.

A Hot Night at the Church

One night I was in a church in Greeley, Colorado, I was a member in its club as I was a member in a number of church clubs in every area that I had lived in, for this is an important facet of American society, deserving close study from the inside. After the religious service in the church ended, boys and girls from among the members began taking part in chants, while others prayed, and we proceeded through a side door onto the dance floor that was connected to the prayer hall by a door, and the Father jumped to his desk and every boy took the hand of a girl, including those who were chanting.

The dance floor was lit with red and yellow and blue lights, and with a few white lamps. And they danced to the tunes of the gramophone, and the dance floor was replete with tapping feet, enticing legs, arms wrapped around waists, lips pressed to lips, and chests pressed to chests. The atmosphere was full of desire. When the minister descended from his office, he looked intently around the place and at the people, and encouraged those men and women still sitting who had not yet participated in this circus to rise and take part. And as he noticed that the white lamps spoiled the romantic, dreamy atmosphere, he set about, with that typical American elegance and levity, dimming them one by one, all the while being careful not to interfere with the dance, or bump into any couples dancing on the dance floor. And the place really did appear to become more romantic and passionate. Then he advanced to the gramophone to choose a song that would befit this atmosphere and encourage the males and the females who were still seated to participate.

And the Father chose. He chose a famous American song called "But Baby, It's Cold Outside," which is composed of a dialogue between a boy and a girl returning from their evening date. The boy took the girl to his home and kept her from leaving. She entreated him to let her return home, for it was getting late, and her mother was waiting but every time she would make an excuse, he would reply to her with this line: but baby, it's cold outside!

And the minister waited until he saw people stepping to the rhythm of this moving song, and he seemed satisfied and contented. He left the dance floor for his home, leaving the men and the women to enjoy this night in all its pleasure and innocence!

The Minister and the Huntresses of Men

Another minister spoke to an Iraqi who was a close friend of mine. The minister asked him about Mary, his classmate at the university, "Why does she no longer come to church?" The minister, apparently, would not care if all the women were absent as long as Mary attended! The Iraqi friend asked the minister about his concern and he answered: "She is attractive, and most of the boys attend only to see her!"

I was speaking to one youth, one of those immoral Arab youths who study in America whom we called "Abu al-Atahiya" after the famous Arab poet of the past, and I do not know whether this angered the old poet or pleased him, and he told me of his girlfriend, as there is a girl for every boy in America, and how she would tear herself from his arms at times to go and sing in the church. If she was late, she would not be spared from the minister's glances and insinuations that "Abu al-Atahiya" played a role in her tardiness in attending the prayer services. This would occur if she attended by herself, without him, but if she were able to bring him along, she would not be blamed nor faulted!

For Them, the End Justifies the Means

And these ministers would say to you: "But we are unable to attract this youth by any other means!"

But none of them asks himself: "What is the value of attracting them to the church, when they rush to it in this way, and spend their time in this manner? Is church attendance a goal in and of itself? Is it not for the edification of feelings and manners? From the minister's point of view, which was made clear by the preceding events, merely going to church is the aim. And this situation makes sense to those who live in America!

But I return to Egypt, and I find those who speak or write about the church in America, even if they have not seen America for a moment, and its role in societal reform, and its activities in purifying the heart and edifying the soul.

But what can I say? Strange things can happen in this world! For God has created all kinds of people and things.

Sexual Primitiveness in America

The American is very primitive in his sexual life, and in his marital and familial relationships. For during my studies of the Holy Bible I have come across a verse in the Old Testament that deals with God's creation of man for the first time and it says: "Males and Females He created them." I came across this verse many times, but it never held for me so nude and lucid a meaning as it did during my time in America.

Sex and Decadence

Human society has long struggled to build and forge sexual mores. It has regulated these relations, emotions, and feelings, and struggled against the coarseness of sensation and the gloominess of natural impulse, in order to let genuine relationships fly about, and free-ranging longings soar high un-fettered, along with all the strong ties around these relationships, in the feelings of individuals, in the life of the family, and in society at large. . . .

This struggle was isolated from life in America at once, and it rose de-void and destitute from every beautification: (males and females) as they were created the first time. Body to body, and female to male. On the basis of bodily needs and motives, relationships are based and ties are established. And from them stretch the rules of behavior, the mores of society, and the ties of families and individuals.

With the temptation of the body alone, devoid of any cover, stripped of all modesty, girls meet boys, and from the strength of the body and its mus-cles the boy obtains the submission of the girl. And the husband obtains his rights, and those rights disappear completely the day that the husband fails to "perform" for one reason or another.

The Appearance of the American Temptress

The American girl is well acquainted with her body's seductive capacity. She knows it lies in the face, and in expressive eyes, and thirsty lips. She knows seductiveness lies in the round breasts, the full buttocks, and in the shapely thighs, sleek legs and she shows all this and does not hide it. She knows it lies in clothes: in bright colors that awaken primal sensations, and in designs that reveal the temptations of the body—and in American girls these are sometimes live, screaming temptations! Then she adds to all this the fetching laugh, the naked looks, and the bold moves, and she does not ignore this for one moment or forget it!

The American Dream Boy

The American boy knows well that the wide, strapping chest is the lure that cannot be denied by any girl, and that her dreams do not fall upon anyone as much as they fall upon the cowboys. A young nurse in a hospi-tal told me very frankly, "I want nothing in the man of my dreams but two strong arms he can really squeeze me with!" And Look magazine ran a sur-vey of several girls of different ages and levels of education and classes around what it called "ox muscles" and the overwhelming majority de-clared their open attraction for boys with ox muscles!

Sex and the Materialism of Life in America

There is no doubt that this fascination with physical strength is indicative of the vitality of this nation and its sensuality. If this fascination were tamed and sublimated, it could lead to the creation of a great art that would remove the gloominess of life and infuse the human spirit with fragrance, and bind the sexes with ties higher and more beautiful than the ties of thirsty bodies, burning passions, and eye-popping sex that beckons through the limbs, and is embodied in motions and gestures. But the nature of life in America, and the circumstance that conditioned the formation of the American people, does not help with any of this, instead it resists and fights it.

The Matter of Sex is Biological in America

The word "bashful" has become a dirty, disparaging word in America. For Americans sexual relations have always conformed to the laws of the jungle. Some Americans philosophize about it, such as one of the girls in the university who once told me: "The matter of sex is not a moral matter at all. It is but a question of biology, and when we look at it from this angle it becomes clear that the use of words like moral and immoral, good and bad, are irrelevant." It may appear that Americans are not only strange, but amusing. Some of them excuse themselves and justify it as one doctoral student did: "We here are occupied with work, and we do not wish to be hindered from it, and we do not have time to invest in feelings. Moreover, books try our nerves, so we wish to do away with this worry to free ourselves for work with relaxed nerves!"

The Americans' Nerves

I did not wish to comment on these statements at the time, for my concern was with knowing how they thought about the matter. But there is nothing in America that indicates relaxed nerves, despite every easy means of life, and all its guaranteed assurances, and every ease and means of expending extra energy.

The Americans Are Free of Humanity

Some of them call this freedom from hypocrisy and facing the truth, but there is a fundamental difference between freedom from hypocrisy and freedom from the components of humanity that separate man from animals. Humanity in its long history was not unaware that sexual desires are normal and true, but it, consciously or unconsciously, struggled to control them, escaping its slavery and distancing themselves from its primitive levels.

Yes, it is a need, so why does humanity shy away from realizing its need? Because it feels inherently that controlling such desires is testament to freedom from slavery and to going beyond the first rungs of humanity's evolution, and that a return to the freedom of the jungle is a gripping slavery and a relapse to the first primitive levels.

Third Episode

Artistic Primitiveness in America

The American is primitive in his artistic tastes, whether in his judgment of art or his own artistic works. Jazz music is his music of choice. It is this music that the savage bushmen created to satisfy their primitive desires, and their desire for noise on the one hand, and the abundance of animal noises on the other. The American's enjoyment of jazz does not fully begin until he couples it with singing like crude screaming. And the louder the noise of the voices and instruments, until it rings in the ears to an unbearable degree, the greater the appreciation of the listeners. The voices of appreciation are raised, and palms are raised in continuous clapping that could deafen ears.

Americans and the Opera

But the American people enjoy the opera, are attracted to the symphony, crowd the ballet, and watch classic theatrical performances to the extent that one might not find a spare seat. It happens that sometimes you may not find a place unless you reserve it days in advance, paying high prices for these shows.

Films and More Films

The cinema is the art of the masses, for it is the art of skill, polish, craft, and accuracy. It is by its nature more dependent upon skill than it is upon artistic spirit, you may be amazed at the American genius in it. Despite this the English, French, Russian, and Italian films remain more elegant than American films, even though they are less skillfully crafted.

The great majority of American films clearly possess simplistic story lines and primitive emotions. They are generally police films and cowboy films. Elevated, brilliant films like "Gone with the Wind," "Wuthering Heights," "Singing Bernadette," and so on, are exceptional in relation to the rest of American production, and what is seen of American films in Egypt or the Arab countries does not illustrate this proportion, because most of them are from the finest, rarest movies of America. Those who visit the theater in America understand this small proportion of quality films.

Natural Scenery in American Art

There is another art in which the Americans have distinguished themselves, for it is more a matter of skill in production than of authentic, elevated art: it is the art of representing natural scenery with colors, as if it were an accurate, true photograph. It is in the museums of marine and land biology, creatures or their preserved bodies are displayed in their natural habitats as if they were real, and the artist's brilliant portrayal of these habitats, combined with artistic design of the scenes, surpasses the limits of amazement.

Primitiveness in Tastes and Preferences

Now we leave these elevated levels of art and feelings to descend to the colors of clothing and the taste of food.

The Clothes of the Americans

Primitiveness of tastes cannot be illustrated more clearly than in these screaming, loud colors, and elaborate large patterns, a lion or a tiger leaping on the chest, an elephant or wild ox prostrating on the back, a naked girl stretched on a necktie from top to bottom, or a palm tree that climbs up it from bottom to top.

So often our commentators do speak of "holiday clothing" in the villages, or the wedding dresses in the village, with their garish, primitive colors that do not match except for the fact that they are the most explosive of colors. I wish these commentators could see the shirts of the boys in America, let alone the clothes of the girls! And as long as commentators speak of tattoos on the gypsies, or in Central Africa, I wish they could see the arms of the American youths and their chests and backs, defiled with green lines, snakes and serpents, naked girls, and trees and jungles. Remember this is happening in modern America, in the New World, in the new universe.

The Food of the Americans

As for their food, that too is very strange. You will attract attention, and cause disbelief, if you request another cube of sugar for the cup of coffee or tea that you drink in America. Sugar is reserved for pickles and salads, while salt, my good sir, is saved for apples and watermelons.

On your plate you will find combined a piece of salted meat, some boiled corn, some boiled peas, and some sweet jam. And on top of all this is what Americans call gravy, which is composed sometimes of fat, vinegar, flour, broth, apples, salt and pepper, and sugar, and water.

Sayyid Qutb Makes Fun of the Americans

We were at the table in one of the cafeterias of the University, when I saw some Americans putting salt on their watermelon. And I was prepared to see these strange fads and also to play jokes on them from time to time. And I said, faking innocence, "I see you sprinkling salt on the watermelon." One of them said, "Yes! Don't you do the same in Egypt?" I said, "No! We sprinkle pepper!" A surprised and curious girl said, "How would that taste?" I said, "You can try for yourself!" She tasted it and said approvingly, "It's tasty!" and so did all the others.

On another day in which watermelon was served, and most of the same people were at the table, I said "Some of us in Egypt use sugar at times instead of pepper." One of them tried it and said, "How tasty!" and so did all the others.

The American Haircut

In summary, anything that requires a touch of elegance is not for the American, even haircuts! For there was not one instance in which I had a haircut there when I did not return home to even with my own hands what the barber had wrought, and fix what the barber had ruined with his awful taste.

America's Role in the World

America has a principal role in this world, in the realm of practical matters and scientific research, and in the field of organization, improvement, production, and management. All that requires mind power and muscle are where American genius shines, and all that requires spirit and emotion are where American naiveté and primitiveness become apparent.

For humanity to be able to benefit from American genius they must add great strength to the American strength. But humanity makes the gravest of errors and risks losing its account of morals, if it makes America its example in feelings and manners.

Of the Virtues of America

All this does not mean that Americans are a nation devoid of virtue, or else, what would have enabled them to live? Rather, it means that America's virtues are the virtues of production and organization, and not those of human and social morals. America's are the virtues of the brain and the hand, and not those of taste and sensibility.

—Translated by Tarek Masoud and Ammar Fakeeh

3.

A Love Tour (1972)

MAHMUD AWAD is an Egyptian journalist who has worked for many years for the daily *al-Akhbar*. His 1972 account *A Love Tour*, is about his journey in a number of countries around the world. On the title page there is a drawing of a naked woman lying down and a minia-ture drawing of a man with a suitcase in hand walking on her body. The man is presumably the writer and the reclining figure stands for the women he came to know and with whom he had sexual li-aisons.

I entered my hotel room and took my clothes off. As I was about to go to bed, there was a knock on the door.

"Who is it?"

"Sammy, this is Liza. Please open the door."

"O.K.," I said reluctantly, "Wait a moment, I have to put my clothes on; I am not wearing anything, not even my pajamas!"

"Open!" said Liza, "You don't have to put anything on; I will spend the night with you."

Liza lay in bed beside me. It was so hot and humid. Liza got up to go to the bathroom, a minute later she came back to lie beside me. Now she was naked. This was the first time I managed to have a good look at Liza. Her eyes were pitch black, glittering in the dark with certain energy, warmth, kindness, and passion. Her hair was blond, straight, generously covering both shoulders. Her skin felt smooth; her breasts were firm, taut as though they were grenades on the brink of exploding.

Liza was tossing and turning beside me, restless, unable to sleep. As she was lying beside me, naked, several times she wiped her face with the back of her hand. She lit a cigarette and puffed at it maybe three times, biting her lips once or twice. She whispered in my ears some inaudible words. She stared at her cupped hand, examining her delicate fingernails then she chose one to bite until she drew blood. When she saw blood oozing from her nails, she got up and went to the bathroom. On her way back to bed she was singing an American song, something like "Let me be ready for you; let me burn with passion; let me smile for you."

Liza must have had a lot to drink tonight. She was drunk, definitely. She was also tense.

"Why don't you hug me?" she asked.

I hugged her.

"Why don't you kiss me?"

I kissed her. Her lips tasted a bit salty but they were full of desire and much tension.

"I want you to . . ." she stopped midway.

It must have been half an hour or even a whole hour, I don't remember. All I remember was that the silence around us was supreme. Yes, silence. Pain. Muffled pain. And many tears.

In a hurt voice, Liza asked me, "Why didn't you . . . ?"

A moment later she repeated the question, "Why Sammy, why didn't you? What is the matter? Don't I appeal to you? The first time I ever asked a man to do that to me and he refused! Why must this happen to me?"

"I don't know," I said.

. . .

Now Liza was calm. Totally calm, in fact. . . . All I knew was this: for me sex should not be a mere entertainment; it should not be had under the influence of alcohol, or after too much partying, or in the name of total freedom. If Liza wanted a hot night of fun, then the fun was over as far as I was concerned. But was Liza really serious about me?

[Two days later]

There was a message for me in my hotel room. It read: "Sammy, I am very, very sorry because I didn't contact you in the last two days. You are always out. . . . I miss you. I don't know how I feel exactly towards you but whatever it is it feels like . . . like . . . love! Liza"

. . .

It is now nine P.M. Two minutes past nine. Three, seven, eight, nine, ten minutes past. There was a knock on the door.

Liza.

An embrace, kisses, tears, love and each one of us was chewing the other!

—Translated by Kamal Abdel-Malek

4.

An American Immigrant (1979)

AHMAD MUSTAFA is an Egyptian-American businessman who moved to the United States in 1967 and lived as an illegal alien in New York City for some years. In his *An American Immigrant* (1979), he recounts with fascinating details his life experiences from rags to riches. The cover of the book shows a man climbing the stripes of the American flag, which are made to look like steps, suggesting that in order to live and succeed in America one ought to work hard in order to climb the American ladder.

Do You Know How to Dance?

Excuse me, dear reader, if I have to give you this piece of advice: before you immigrate to the Unites States you should learn how to dance. This advice does not mean that I am calling for debauchery or the loosening of your morals, or for you to be frivolous and waste your time in something other than making money. No. What I mean to say is that dancing in America is a language that you need to learn in the same manner you need to learn English. You learn dancing in order to become a modern man capable of living permanently in a new society. Besides, during your stay in the United States you may have to go out dancing in a disco with some of your American friends or you may get invited to a party where everyone will be dancing except you because you don't know how. In this case you will end up alone in a corner while your girlfriend or your wife is dancing with people you don't know. Dancing may also be the way you'll get a fabulous job. Imagine for a moment this scenario: you are somewhere dancing with a young woman or a distinguished lady; you impress your dancing partner and she in turn introduces you to a VIP who in turn will give you a fabulous job. Or you may go to a disco and meet a wealthy lady who'll like you and marry you and you will become a millionaire, as it has happened to some men. At any rate this is just my advice to you; take it or leave it. You may ask me: "Why didn't you learn how to dance while you were living in the Unites States?" My answer is: "I wish I did while I was living in New York for so many years. Had I learned how to dance then I wouldn't have written this book and you would have read in the newspapers about my marriage to an American millionaire."

My Experiences in America

Excuse me, dear reader, for writing you an entire passage on the experiences I have had in America. I lived in New York, the city that is deafening, annoying, scary, and beautiful all at the same time. It is also the city that welcomed me at the beginning of my life, a life that was full of misery, misfortune, tears, and sighs.

Later, the city saw me depart with a smile, full of hope and joy; hoping that I will return to it again some day.

The point of writing these particular memories of my life is to narrate to you some of my experiences in the United States of America. If you travel to the United States without immigrant status, you can learn from my life story and extract wisdom from my experiences!

I left my great country, Egypt, after the 1967 war. I escaped from Egypt by pretending to seek medical treatment and to pursue my studies, but I never planned to return.

Nobody knew this except for three people and they were my dearest friends. I wrote one of them secretly giving him the responsibility of taking care of my apartment in Cairo during my absence.

I decided to travel to the city of New York and I hurriedly prepared everything in 48 hours!

I knew nothing about New York and I do not know why I chose it out of all the cities or states in America. All my thinking was centered on leaving Egypt. My decision to leave was based on advice from some of my close friends, who occupied important government posts at the time. I used to work as a press secretary for one of the government ministers as well as a journalist for the *Al-Akhbar* newspaper.

I took the plane from Cairo to New York. I spent the trip thinking about my unknown fate in America because I hardly knew anyone there. I relied only on God.

All my thoughts were on my escape from Egypt. It had been rumored in all circles that I was against the government. It was said I was spreading harsh political jokes that made fun of the president and the government.

Once I escaped from the grip of the authorities in Egypt, from their questioning and torture, I started wondering about my future.

What shall I do in America? What is my fate there? The questions were circling around in my head like the buzzing of bees as they roam around their hive.

I decided to leave all these questions, which were filling my mind, to destiny and God. I occupied myself with reading some newspapers and magazines that were on the airplane. Then I turned to engage in conversation with the man who sat next to me on the plane.

When the plane landed at Kennedy International Airport in New York, I was impressed by the airport's organization, luxury, and class. I started looking about and I went to claim my baggage. Then I stood in line with other people who were on the plane with me to have our passports checked by the official at the airport. My turn came and I went up to the official and handed him my passport. He looked at it and then he looked at all my baggage. He told me in his American accent, which I was hearing for the first time, "Wait there!" pointing to the side of the airport. So I went where he told me. After half an hour, once he had finished looking at the last passport, he came to me and said as he was inspecting my passport, "Why did you come with an entry visa without a departure date? Are you planning to reside here permanently?"

I said to him, innocently, "Yes."

He smiled mockingly and said, "Your country is with the Communists and we don't want Communists in our country!"

I replied, "I am not a Communist. I am against Communism."

He said, "You have to return to your country. Wait here!" He left me and went to an office in the airport where the man who seemed to be in charge was sitting. He spoke to him and then came back with him. I was trembling with fear at the thought of being returned to Egypt. I didn't know what would happen to me. The customs chief came toward me asking, "Why did you come to New York? Don't you know that relations between your country and our country are bad? What will you do here if you're not an immigrant?"

Before I answered his questions, I heard a voice calling me from within the airport. I looked toward the source of the voice and I saw an American friend of mine standing and waiting for me. I had contacted him from the airport in Cairo through the travel agency, to inform him of my arrival in New York.

My friend made his way past the officials in the airport and entered the customs area where I was standing with the customs chief. He approached us and introduced himself. He then asked me what the complications were, so I informed him of what had occurred. I told him that there was a possibility that I could be deported to Egypt.

My friend took a card out of his pocket and the officials looked at it and he said to them, "He's a journalist." He asked that I be let out of the airport under his responsibility, and that he would take care of the problem with an immigration official in the city. A phone call was made and I left the airport with a two-month visa!

My American friend took my luggage and put it in his car, and we took off to the city. While driving, he said, "I have rented a room for you in a youth hostel until you take care of your business and find a job." He took me there and then left me.

I had hoped that this friend would search for a job for me. He actually tried, but he failed in all his attempts. He failed because I was not a legal immigrant. According to American law, I did not have the right to work in any field. Secondly, relations between Egypt and the United States were rather bad and there was no diplomatic representation for Egypt. Thirdly, Americans thought Egypt had joined the Soviet Union and that all Egyptians were Communists! Finally, all American supervisors in any company were scared of being responsible for employing an Egyptian illegal alien.

My American friend informed me of all this as he presented his excuses for this embarrassing and difficult situation I was in now.

The world seemed to cave in on me and I was incapable of swallowing any kind of food or drink. Thinking about my future occupied me day and night. I did not sleep. I cried, "What shall I do? Should I commit suicide? My belief in God forbids me from thinking about committing suicide. Who should I turn to?" I went out of my room in the youth hostel crying. I walked in the street until I found a cafeteria. I walked in and sat on one of the seats in the room as tears kept pouring out of my eyes.

A young man who was sitting on a nearby stool approached me, speaking in Arabic, and said, "Are you Egyptian?"

I looked at him and said, "Yes . . ."

He replied, "I am Lebanese and my wife is Egyptian. My name is Muhammed." He asked, "Why are you crying?"

I said to him, "I'm in a mess," and I told him my story. The young man smiled at me as he laid his hand on my shoulder and said, "Don't worry. I'll give you work tomorrow!"

I started chatting with this Lebanese man about my departure from Egypt and what I used to do. After he heard my true story, he said, "Work here is not shameful. I mean, any job a human does is not shameful. Shame is when you beg from people or stay without a job. There is not a single person in America without a job." Then he paid for my drink and said, "Let's go."

I asked, "Where?"

He said, "To my home so I can introduce you to my brother who works as the manager of one of the nightclubs in New York."

. . .

[At the nightclub, the author started his job as a waiter, he was very nervous because he had no experience whatsoever. Under pressure from his Lebanese friend he had to pretend that he had worked as an assistant manager in a famous Cairo hotel.]

My Lebanese friend took my hand and walked me to the end of the nightclub. Pointing to a corner that had five tables, he said to me: "This is your section." Then he left me. A moment later he came back to say to me: "Don't stand with your hands tied like this. Do something! You must show the boss that you are doing something. Move the chairs around, tidy the table, rearrange the forks and the knives." I did what he asked me to do. After a while patrons started to arrive. I walked around pretending that I was a very experienced waiter, a pro who knows the ins and outs of this profession. I seated four patrons in my section until it was almost full. It was then that I started to panic.

I went up to one of the tables to take the orders. Each one of the patrons ordered an alcoholic drink. One said to me: "I would like to have a Manhattan." I said to myself "What a shitty beginning!" I knew then as I do now that Manhattan is the name of the financial district in New York, so what was that guy talking about ordering Manhattan? He must have been drinking lots of whiskey before coming to the nightclub. He must have had too much to drink. I went to my Lebanese friend and said to him, "The guy over there is really drunk; he wants me to bring him 'Manhattan!'" The Lebanese friend laughed and said to me that a Manhattan was a drink.

. . .

I worked for a week at the nightclub. I used to start at 6:00 P.M. to prepare everything and finish at 4:00 A.M. When after a week I went to get my paycheck, one of the owners of the nightclub looked at me and said, "What money are you talking about? We owe you no money."

I was taken aback by this answer so I said to him, "I have worked for a whole week and I need to be paid for my work."

He said, "Are you a resident? Do you have a work permit?"

I said, "No, my friend must have told you."

So he said to me, "People like you without papers or work permits work for free; the tips they get are more than enough. Do you want to work or do you want to quit? Or do you want me to call the police?"

The word, "police" frightened me since it was illegal for me to work anywhere. If I were caught I would be deported right away. I left the nightclub in tears while cursing my Lebanese friend, the owners of the nightclub, and the drunken patrons.

—Translated by Kamal Abdel-Malek and May Kassem

5.

New York 80 (1980?)

YUSUF IDRIS was the most famous short story writer and playwright in Egypt. His collections of short stories and plays depict the plight of the underprivileged and the conflict between individuals and societal pressures. His *Cheapest of Nights* (1954), *City Dregs* (1957), and *The Stooges* (1964) are among his best works and they have been translated into several foreign languages including English, French, and Russian. His *New York 80*, excerpted here, is a fictionalized encounter with an American "call girl," based on his actual visit to the United States in the early 1980s. *New York 80* is a telling description of Arab attitudes toward America by one of the most famous Arab writers. Idris died in 1991.

He: Excuse me madam, by the way, is this the right way to talk to women? Or should I say "Ma'am"?

There was a surprised look from her, then astonishment, then slight annoyance.

She: And why not? As you like, say "madam" if you wish, or "ma'am." Why not? That's the custom here.

He: Madam, it is obvious that you are . . . you are . . .

She: Yes, yes, to save both of us time, I'm a call girl. Do you know what that means? To save myself more time, I'm what they call a prostitute.

Her answer was not a surprise to him, except that it had happened very quickly. His brain worked as fast as lightning. He repeated the question and the answer several times, not to make sure, but rather to comprehend the situation. After he comprehended it, he reprimanded himself because he was the one who was embarrassed now. So he raised his head to face her. Her head was at a 45-degree angle. As for his eyes, they were in their eye sockets, but their angle was aimed upward. It seemed as though he was seeing through the white portion of his eyes.

He (to himself): A prostitute? Why do they call everything here by its real name? Are they not ashamed? In any case, we are more civilized than they are. You may call it hypocrisy or whatever, but it is still more acceptable than the blatant truth and the words mean exactly the same. Prostitute! The word is ugly in any language, even in French. After all, Sartre's virtuous prostitute is still a prostitute.

He saw bulletin boards all over the place and images of prostitutes were bombarding him as strongly as the New York rain.

But here is the truth that must be stated: the lady he spoke to did not show any connection with prostitution. She wore stylish eyeglasses, not sunglasses, and he adores women in eyewear. The eyes of the woman who wears glasses may provide insightful information about that woman, from the tiniest detail to the most intimate secret with regard to her attraction to a man.

Prostitute!

She must be a novice in this illegal profession; it seemed that she had only started yesterday. What was certain was that inside this young woman was a strong magnet that pulled her toward the male gender, even before the man had time to be attracted to her.

He: Madam or ma'am as you say in America, I would like to tell you something clearly. I was sitting here before you. I noticed that once you arrived you searched the place with your glasses, and despite the fact that most of the seats were empty, you chose to sit at the other side of the same bench as me. I also noticed that the three men sitting opposite to me had left the seats next to them empty so as to try to lure you into sitting next to them. I watched you closely, until I could bear it no longer and pitied you. I thanked God for not creating me a woman who was a slave to men. What was the name of that last man you spoke to? He was very rude and only worthy of getting slapped. I noticed how he tried to tempt you by continually stating the name of the famous worldwide company where he worked.

She (interrupting): And he smelled.

He: Something very upsetting and disgusting. But again you are free, and you have chosen a life in which you do not choose men but they choose you. You are free, but your freedom will have to stop now because I tell you so. I also noticed that you rejected some men even though they had very big wallets and big egos, because you noticed me. In fact, you looked more than once toward me. I would like to be very honest with you. I despise your type. I cannot imagine how a woman could sell her body, no matter how desperate she is for money. It does not seem that you are dying of hunger, but instead there is a very expensive ring worth at least a thousand dollars on your finger. I am disgusted with your type. I despise it and I feel like vomiting just looking at it. To be more honest with you I am not waiting for anyone, not a man or a woman, but instead I am very tired and my sitting at the edge of this bench is very comfortable for me and I do not intend to give it up.

She is puzzled; she listens; she understands; she does not get upset. It is as though the words were not intended for her. "Why won't she leave?" he thought to himself.

He (continuing): I despise your kind to such a great extent that no brain can imagine, certainly not yours; yours is a brain that does not react to these insults. Honestly, between us, you rejected the men before me because, I don't know why, you had your eyes on me. In all honesty I say to you that I would prefer to go out with a gorilla than to go out with you or even speak to you for that matter. It is all a matter of morality to me, and I consider women of your type to be my enemy. If I were a murderer by nature, I would have killed you all. So then, I am not your customer and I will never be one. So either you leave this place, or you look for another customer, since it bothers me to know that I may cause you, even a person like you, some disappointment (by turning you down).

She faced him completely, with strength. To him, professional prostitutes had faces smothered with excessive makeup and wore wigs or dressed their hair in such a way that would attract attention. This was how he would recognize these prostitutes even from a distance, whether in Cairo or any other city in the world. This lady who was sitting beside him, however, had but a little makeup on and her face was completely normal. She had a seductive look to her appearance but it was not intentional. If he had met her in another place he would have thought she was the vice president of the public relations office in the United Nations (vice president and not president because she was definitely between 25 to 30.) There was no explicit, inviting smile on her face for a customer. She cared little about what the gentleman said and was disdainful and haughty. She remained calm and respectful as though she were proud of a respectable profession she had.

Then with an unpretentious smile that matched her glamorless matte lipstick, she responded to him by saying: Then I should understand from what you said that you would like me to leave?

He: Of course not, I did not say that.

She: Then why don't you leave my bench?

He: This is neither yours nor mine, it is owned by the bar, and I have no intention of changing my place.

She: Then the problem is that you do not like whores.

He: Neither them nor their likes, and not even the ones who accept love for the purpose of being taken out to dinner or given a gift. It is a sad, sad thing; it is the sort of behavior that does not behoove a human being.

He realizes she is using the soft and gentle side of her tongue. No. It cannot be that she began her career just yesterday, as I had thought. She is a master of the trade. The next sentence will drag the answer out of his mouth even if he tries to resist. So what does he do? This was the first time in his life not only to sit shoulder-to-shoulder with a prostitute, but also to converse with one. In his own country and during his many travels he came across many women, amateur and professional types, who would offer themselves to him, either for gifts or for money. But in all cases they were shy, sensitive. Once the signs of rejection appeared on his face, either they immediately left him alone, looked to the side, looked for another customer, or even just stood up and left the place. But this woman was in a league of her own. Either this woman was very confident of herself, or she was the type that does not get embarrassed and tries to lessen the degree of her craftiness. Or it may be that she had some time to waste. Or, and this possibility appealed to his pride, she preferred him to others or wanted to make him her favorite man. In either case, man, do not think so highly of yourself.

She: Honestly, why do you not like prostitution?

He: Because I believe that love, even the physical type, should not be bought.

She gave a long, spontaneous laugh. A laugh that did not resemble any of those he had encountered. It is more reserved than the laughs of Cairo's beauties in their posh Gizira club, at least it originated from the heart. Following this, was the repetition of his previous sentence:

He: Because I believe that love, even the physical type, should not be bought.

She laughed one more time. The amount of sarcasm in this second laugh was clearer this time, but still it carried an underlying deeper meaning, as though she were laughing at an idiot or some idiotic conversation.

He: *Effendim?*

She: Yes, what are you saying?

He: *Effendim?*

She: What language is that?

He: A language.

She: Greek?

He: No.

She: Polish?

He: No.

She: What country are you from?

He did not want to be lured. Her tongue was very slippery and because of his aggressive tone her appetite was increasing more and more. It seems she was planning some mischief. This was incredible, what he was witnessing. This woman would sell the one precious thing valuable to a woman. She treated her body as though it were a sack of potatoes or a bunch of radishes. His hatred for her was rising up his esophagus, and filling his throat. His smell and the smell of her perfume mixed with each other to produce a smell similar to the grocery and meat markets in Paris; now that odious smell was threatening to turn into a smell similar to that of the leather-tanning piers at the port of Alexandria.

He: *Effendim?*

She: What country are you from?

He (to himself): Answer her you, you timid man, with a rude voice so that she may leave you alone.

He: From a place in this world.

She: And what do you do?

He: Any job.

She: And what do you mean "any job?" Every human being works at one thing or another. What is your line of work?

He: A job that is respectful, like the jobs of these clean-shaven people here around you in the bar.

She: A businessman?

He: A man, without business.

She: Why are you trying to be vague?

He: Because I do not trust you.

She: Even with respect to your line of work?

He: Even with respect to my work.

She faced him straight on. O Lord, she was the prettiest one of all, the most beautiful woman, not only in the bar but anywhere. He has not seen anyone so beautiful in such a long time let alone argued with and was obnoxious to a woman of such beauty. No, it was not only the green eyes, the golden hair, or the Brigitte Bardot mouth but also her skin color, which was a very light tannish red. Her bodily features were astonishing, created, no doubt, by a very intelligent and sensitive mind. This was a beauty that the Creator fashioned with pleasure, and the created then went on to enhance her own beauty with attractive intelligence. If you glanced at her you were immediately drawn to her eyes. A young woman who he has to love; a young woman for whose sake he would neglect all his priorities; a young woman for whose sake and for the sake of all who are like her, men become lost and lose sight of what is important.

But nonetheless, she sells her body. A masterpiece put up for sale.

Suddenly, a wolf-like desire seized him to stare and observe, just like the Egyptian women on Oxford Street window-shopping, but with no intention of buying.

—Translated by Kamal Abdel-Malek and Charles Khoury

6.

America: The Jeans and the Switchblade (1989)

MUHAMMAD HASAN AL-ALFI is an Egyptian reporter who lived for
a year and a half in the United States. He visited many states and be-
friended many Americans from all walks of life. Some of the chapters of his book deal with Halloween, UFOs and aliens, ESP, a visit
to Alcatraz prison, violent crimes in America, capital punishment in
America, cloning, and Cairo-Washington relations. The cover of his
book has a picture of a male punk with a Mohawk haircut, sticking
out his tongue.

It was October 31st, ten minutes after midnight. American police were
roaming the streets, nervously, cautiously, at times slithering their way
like snakes. The police knew very well what to expect that night. News-
casts also warned people about what was to happen that night and made
references to the incidents of the past year. The state police were ready for
any violence that might break out during the annual satanic celebration.

Droves of black and white young people wore torn clothes in loud colors, clothes that did not always cover their bodies. They loitered around;
some were running; some singing very loudly or rather shouting. They
danced or stood still like statues I saw at the Museum of Fine Arts in Min-
nesota. . . . The policemen—riding white or black horses that glistened in
the dark because they were recently washed—were watching the scene on
the streets. There was no crime or fire yet.

A boy and a girl wore horror masks that concealed their beautiful
human features. The boy wore a mask of a blood-sucking vampire, and the
girl wore a mask of the princess of darkness with blood oozing from both
sides of her blue-colored mouth . . .

The famous American writer Stephen King, the prince of the horror
story, is the favorite writer among Americans that night (Halloween). He

is a prolific writer of horror fiction. Four years ago we Egyptians saw a horror movie based on his novel, *The Shining* . . .

This is what had happened in three major cities (Los Angeles, San Diego, and Long Beach) that night: major fires, shootings, a wild party of 100,000 men, women, and children on Hollywood Street. . . . In fact, things got out of hand and the revelers went on a rampage and damaged windows of stores and looted stocks of wine and beer. A young woman was raped in the melee and three policemen were injured and taken to the hospital.

It is a mad, mad world.

—Translated by Kamal Abdel-Malek

7.

America for Sale (1991)

MAHMUD IMARA is an Egyptian-American, born in 1952, who immigrated first to France in 1974, then to the United States in the 1987 where he settled in Florida. He studied law at Cairo University and economics at the Sorbonne. His book, *America for Sale,* has on its cover a picture of an American cowboy with the typical hat, bandana, boots, and a cigarette dangling from his mouth. Some of the topics covered in *America for Sale* are: New York as the city of freedom and vagabondage, American television, the Kennedys, American farms, the bitterness of exile, and Disneyworld.

[Observations about life in America]

- It is said that a few people immigrated to America in search of God, but the overwhelming majority of immigrants came in search of gold.
- Everything in America is for sale. With the dollar you can buy anything: railway stations, airports, churches, cemeteries with the dead buried in them. Everything. Everything except wives and kids. But wives in America can sell their husbands.
- Everywhere in America you will find ads about items for sale: in the streets, on corners, on houses, on cars, and even airplanes. Newspapers devote about 70 percent of their space for ads. On TV, ads are the one and the only revenue for TV channels. Whole channels are sometimes totally devoted to ads; the ads are run for 24-hours-a-day and people can buy with a simple phone call during which they provide their credit cards numbers and the next day they get the merchandise by mail.
- If you happen to stop at a traffic light the car driver waiting next to you may ask you if you want to sell your car. At the next traffic light you and he may agree on a price then at the rest area you deliver your car to him and receive the money and you hitchhike home.

- I once bought a newspaper in which I saw the following ad:

A Husband for Sale

A wife is putting her husband up for sale for a reasonable price. He is friendly and won't bite. He owns many pairs of jeans, shoes, and shirts. He also owns full hunting gear with a trained hunting dog. But he is out of town from April to October every year.

A week later I read this follow-up to the ad:

The wife (44-years-old), a nurse, received 60 phone calls from women interested in buying the husband. But the wife changed her mind about selling him. The wife found out that the reason why there was such a demand was because the husband owned a hunting dog and she decided she could not do without the dog!

- "An Airport for Sale," I saw this sign and became interested to find out more about it.
  "How much?" I asked.
  The secretary pointed out a man on her right who had a tattoo of a lion on one arm, a naked woman on the other. He had his hair tied in a ponytail with a hairband.
  "How much do you want for the airport?" I asked him.
  He told me that it was his wife who was selling the airport and that he was merely an employee.
- "Buy an acre on the moon for only ten dollars! Get a round-trip ticket . . . to the moon to visit your new property. For info. call 1–900–555–5555, $2 per minute."
- "A Church for Sale." My American friend James went to inquire. The clergyman asked him if he could still keep 20 percent of the church's income and if he wanted to pay in cash . . .
- "Cemeteries for Sale." That was so spooky we did not inquire about it.
- "A Highway for Sale." It was the only highway that connected this American town and another in the west. The ad mentioned the highway had four lanes and that the allowed speed on it was 65 miles-per-hour . . .
- There was land for sale, property for sale, an island for sale, America itself for sale. But who would buy America? Americans or foreigners?

—Translated by Kamal Abdel-Malek

III

America: The Dream and the Reality,
the American as an Example to Emulate

8.

America in the Eyes of an Easterner,
Or Eight Years in the United States (1924)

PHILIP K. HITTI was a well-known American academic of Syro-Lebanese origins. He taught for many years at Princeton University where he established one of America's first programs in Middle Eastern studies. He was a noted historian of Arab and Islamic history and published numerous books in the field including *History of the Arabs,* which has appeared in many editions. He published an account of his life in America first in a serialized form in *al-Hilal* literary magazine then in a book in 1924 under the title, *America in the Eyes of an Easterner, Or Eight Years in the United States,* with a preface by Emile Zaydan, then editor of *al-Hilal.* Some of the topics in the book are: the vitality of Americans, American efficiency, the spirit of cooperation, American inventiveness and resourcefulness, and the American democratic spirit.

The first thing that attracts your attention as a visitor to America is how extremely lively Americans are. The minute you arrive by boat in New York, the U.S. port, you will be greeted with the sight of a series of skyscrapers on the horizon, tall buildings with 50 or 60 floors. You will feel as though you have arrived in a country whose inhabitants are giants among men. When you enter the city and walk among the people, you will be struck by how eager Americans are to go to their work, how quick their pace is, and how active and energetic they are. You will then realize that you are not in a country like others, and you are not among a people like others, but rather among a people superior in their qualities, distinguished in their vitality, and unique in their abundance of energy. The matchless skyscrapers, the quick pace of life, the ability to focus on one's work, are none other than manifestations of the dynamism of a nation that is full of youth and pulsating with tremendous energy.

. . .

The first thing you are told the minute you step out of the boat [upon your arrival on the U.S. shores] and while you are still on the board that connects the boat with land—and that separates the Old from the New World—is, "Step lively!" It is a command that you'll hear time and again from the lips of train and bus conductors all over the country as though stepping lively were the slogan of the new life in this new land.

Whereas the command you are bound to hear in Eastern countries is, "Take your time!" or "Watch out!" or "Don't trip!" One can see that these Eastern and Western commands reveal the difference in the whole outlook on life between Easterners and Americans.

"Hurry is Satan's way," is a proverb that is unknown to Americans. For the American eats in a hurry, walks in a hurry, works in a hurry, lives his life in a hurry, dies in a hurry, and even is buried in a hurry, a hurry like the speed of the turning wheels. This is what observers of the American scene have said about America and what many French, British, German, Italian, or Spanish writers have noted.

The tailor in America hangs a sign on his shop that says that he irons and mends your clothes, "While you wait." The shoemaker says that he can mend your shoes while you wait in his shop. Many restaurants serve fast food with signs such as "Quick Lunch." In America you can sit at the barber's chair and have one man cut your hair, another prune your fingernails, while a third shines your shoes. Three operations are conducted simultaneously on one person.

One of the amusing anecdotes I heard in America, which reveals this national trait of doing things in a hurry, tells of an insurance salesman who wanted to sell a life insurance policy to a resident Cuban businessman. The American insurance salesman said, "If you are to fall off from this window, an insurance check will reach your wife before you hit the ground of the street." Amazed, the Cuban businessman said to him, "Suppose I hit the ground but I am not hurt, what will you do in this case?" The insurance salesman replied, "Well, a telegram will have been sent to stop the payment!"

. . .

Love of Work

Love of work, earnestness, and perseverance are some of the signs that show American energy and liveliness. Work is the fundamental American ethos. Old and young people, men and women, rich and poor, they all work several hours a day, from eight in the morning until five in the evening. Each one has his own work. Some work at home, others in the market, or in the office, or in the laboratory, or in the store. Everyone works; none is lazy. If you do not enjoy work for its own sake, then you will not have a happy life in America.

"With the sweat of your brow, you shall earn your living," is a [Biblical] verse that originated in the East but is followed to the letter in America.

Edison once was asked about genius, if you are looking for an example of genius then Edison is the one. Edison replied, "Genius is 99 percent perspiration and 1 percent inspiration." Edison's words reveal the American spirit.

In our East, the homemaker steps out of her home and buys food for breakfast and gathers some wood to fuel her stove. Her house is heated and lit by the rays of the sun during the day, and receives moonbeams at night so that it does not need any artificial light. But here in America a price, a big price, has to be paid for everything you eat, drink, wear, and use to have your place lit or heated. Because this is the case in America then it becomes necessary to work in order to earn your living and pay for your own expenses. No neighbor will aid you, and no relative will have pity on you. If you don't work, you will simply perish.

In America the woman works, if not as a homemaker then as a doctor, a lawyer, a teacher, or a secretary. Whenever you enter an office or a store in America you will find a secretary, typing business letters or keeping accounts. The secretary in my office had a high school diploma; her father was a big businessman, perfectly capable of financially taking care of his daughter. But it is the American principle that stipulates that a daughter should work in order to pay for some of her expenses and as a consequence will feel that she is an independent individual, self-respected, and respected by others.

During the war [World War I] women were employed in factories, railways, and public buses as guards, drivers, and conductors. You will find women working everywhere you go, even in churches, some churches have male as well as female clergy. One of the Christian denominations, the Christian Science, always ordains a preacher (they call him reader) with a female aide. I once got acquainted with a woman from Brooklyn who told me that she worked as a clergywoman and asked me to come one Sunday to hear her sermon.

Students work. No matter how wealthy a student's father is, he is not expected to pay for all his son's expenses. The son is expected to work during his spare time in order to pay for some of his needs. In every university in America there is an official who helps students find jobs, all sorts of jobs. You may see one student working as a waiter, another cleaning toilets, another collecting wood [for fuel and heating], another removing snow from the front doors. I remember a student at Columbia University who used to wash cars every night from seven until midnight.

Once I entered a barber's shop in one of the seaside resorts in Massachusetts. I found some large medical books on the table and I said to myself, what on earth could these medical and surgical tomes have to do with this barber. When I inquired with the barber, he said to me, "I am in my fourth year; I have shaved my way through college!" And he named his medical school; it was one of the top schools in the country.

A female cousin of mine lived in a small town in West Virginia. Once when I went to visit her, I saw a painter who was dressed in dirty clothes painting the walls on a high ladder. My cousin called him and introduced him to me. I really did not see the point of all of this, since I did not have anything in common with him, until my cousin introduced him by saying that he was one of the top students in his class at the University of West Virginia and that he was to graduate soon. This young man, as it were, "painted his way through college!"

In American eyes there is no shame in any kind of work. What is truly shameful for the Americans is to be unemployed or lazy.

Macadeau, President Wilson's son-in-law and the secretary of finance during the war, spent millions of dollars on loans to the Allies and on the U.S. Army. Once the war was over, he resigned his position because his salary was not enough to pay for his family's expenses. Instead he accepted work as a lawyer for a group of actors, among whom were Douglas Fairbanks and Charlie Chaplin. While he was in this position he was nominated as a candidate for the presidency to succeed his father-in-law, President Wilson.

You may hear wealthy Americans boasting about how they started their careers with menial, low-paying jobs. The incumbent president Warren Harding, for example, was once a carriage driver. (Since this book was written President Harding died on August 2, 1923.)

The rich work. When Easterners think of rich Americans such as Ford, Morgan, or Rockefeller, they imagine them having a good time taking a promenade, or sitting in a café or bar and savoring the joys of life. There is nothing further from the truth. I bet that if you went to see one of them, you would find him in his office hard at work, poring over business letters and correspondence to his partners, planning his future projects.

The old work. The ideal thing for an Easterner is to become rich enough to retire and rest. For him that would be heaven on earth. I noticed that many Easterners when they reach 50 they think that their life is over and their work finished. For an American, on the other hand, if one's work is terminated, then one's life is over.

President Wilson is now 70 years old. His presidency came to an end on March 2 of last year and on March 3 he declared that he had opened a law firm in Washington, D.C. He suffered from hemiplegia toward the end of his tenure in office and signs of this disease can still be seen in his face and arm. By working he does not seek to make more money for he has made more than enough. He does not seek to be famous; if he did not obtain fame as the occupant of the White House, it would be absurd to seek fame now a mere lawyer. But President Wilson believes, as do many of his compatriots, that without work his life will come to an end; he simply does not wish to be one of the living dead.

Strenuous Life

President Theodore Roosevelt was a living example of American energy and dynamism. For this reason he was well respected by people of his generation and greatly admired as a contemporary hero by his compatriots. His life was a strenuous life, this is an apt description of it. This is illustrated throughout his career: as the commander of volunteer soldiers in the war in Cuba, as the governor of New York, as the president of the United States, as a hunter of wild animals in Africa, as an explorer in the Amazon, and as the editor of the magazine *Outlook* and the newspaper the *Kansas City Star.* Roosevelt is the man who coined the phrase, "strenuous life" as the most apt description of American life, which French writers translate as "*la vie intense.*"

Hard work or the strenuous life does not cause death. Otherwise the longevity rate in the United States in 1900 would not have been as high as 35 years, or 36 as it is recorded this year by the medical inspector of the state of New York. Whereas the longevity rate in India is 12 years, and in Cairo 15 years as it was stated by the *American Geographical Magazine* in one of its issues last year.

Comparison between the
Easterner and the American

The Easterner imagines Paradise as a place of rest for the righteous where they will retire from work, enjoy the quiet and serenity of the place, and the most they will do is pray and sing hymns. As for the American, if he is at all as religious as the Easterner, he will imagine paradise as a place of work and noise, full of offices and establishments, where there is an assigned job for everyone, and everyone has to work and work hard, nonstop.

In my view herein lies the difference between the Eastern and Western psyche. The Easterner is an idealist, a romantic; his main concern is with the afterlife and his salvation in the afterlife. The American, on the other hand, is a materialist, a pragmatist; his main concern is with this world and with how to improve it. For this reason, the Easterner has become the world's teacher of literature (or good manners) and its spiritual master. The American, on the other hand, has become the master of the world's land and the commander of the seas.

Were the American to stand and watch the waters that separate Brooklyn from the rest of New York, he would think of building a bridge on which trains and cars can pass, carrying people and goods from one side to another. But were the Easterner to stand and watch the same waters, he would probably compose a poem. Were the American to watch Niagara Falls, he would think of how to convert the water power into electric power with which the adjacent towns would be lit and trains and cars be run. As for the Easterner, he would probably sing a traditional song in honor of the beautiful falls.

—Translated by Kamal Abdel-Malek

9.

The World in America (1926)

AMIR BOQTOR is an American-educated Egyptian who worked as the registrar of the American University in Cairo (AUC) during the 1920s. He studied at Columbia University in New York where he received his B.A. and M.A. degrees. He visited the United States again in 1924. During this short stay, he studied American pedagogical methods and met with many educators. He dedicated his book, *The World in America* (1926), to Dr. Robert Maclennan, the dean of the Faculty of Arts and Sciences at AUC with these words: "I offer you my book about America, your beloved and beautiful country, the cradle of freedom and the homeland of democracy." Some of the topics covered in this book are: the Statue of Liberty, the wonders of American inventions, the wireless, Henry Ford, the scientific experiments in America, the American press, democracy in America, Syrian-Americans, women's awakening in America, the differences between the customs and manners of the East and the West, leisure in America, family life, co-ed education, the Museum of Natural History in New York, and so on.

Now I will go over the differences between us and Westerners, particularly the Americans among them.

Westerners are more modest in their tastes than us Easterners. They prefer quiet so if they talk, they talk in a soft voice so that they do not disturb others around them. If they have weddings or funerals, no one hears their noise on these occasions. As for Easterners, they shout when they talk, their music in weddings is very loud, and they fill the earth with their wailing and crying during the funeral of their loved ones. Westerners prefer soft lights in their homes in order to enjoy quiet. When we talk we gesticulate with hands, heads, and eyes something that Westerners dislike. (I warn all Egyptian travelers to America against engaging in these practices there.) They dislike loud colors in clothes and furniture, whereas we like them.

Their furniture is simple and tastefully situated in their rooms; ours is too much, overcrowding our rooms.

If you say to your Western host while at a meal that you have had enough, he would not offer you seconds. But in our country you are obliged to eat more than you wish just for the sake of your host. Unlike the case in our country, here in America they drink tea, coffee, soup, and other liquid food without slurping. (Here I must urge you not only to desist from practicing this hateful habit but to fight it and to warn all Egyptians against it.)

Entertainment is essential to Westerners and only secondary for us. For them time is money; for us time is worthless. In America they are accustomed to doing things very efficiently, very meticulously; here in Egypt our slogan is "Never mind!" (ma'alishsh). Americans regard work as something honorable, something that would give one a sense of dignity; for us work is degrading. Americans think first then form an opinion; we, on the other hand, form an opinion first then think the matter over and that is the reason why our opinions and beliefs are based on old traditions, customs, and nonsensical absurdities.

They are not afraid of candidness whereas it frightens us and we try our best to avoid it. We do not, for example, acknowledge that we are poor when we truly are; in fact, we pretend we are not and spend more on appearances than on our real needs.

We exaggerate in complimenting and praising others, and waste time, to such an extent that our compliments become at times sheer hypocrisy and insincerity. For Americans, compliments are based on honest appraisal and they are brief.

In our homes we do not care to wear nice clothes when we sit down for our meals, in fact we remain in our sleeping gowns; Americans on the other hand sit down for their meals, dressed up and with their hair combed.

Americans avoid becoming overweight, especially the women among them. As for us, excess weight is one of the ingredients of beauty. In our country people care much about wearing expensive clothes and perfumes with strong scents; in America they simply dislike all artificial scents. They also do not care about clothes as much as they care about their health, diet, and exercise. For Americans, having a straight, full, and healthy figure is the most important aspect of looking good.

Here in our country we cherish the past and follow in the footsteps of our ancestors and for this reason our actions are unchanged and unvaried; in America, they respect that which from the past may help them in building the present and benefiting the future, but at the same time they detest things old and worn out. The following anecdote illustrates very well what

I have just stated: "A newspaper correspondent once handed his editor a piece of paper with the following story: 'A rabid dog bit a man in such-and-such neighborhood and the man was taken to hospital.' The editor crumbled the piece of paper and threw it in the correspondent's face saying, "Hey buster, what's new in this story? Go to the inner city, to the side streets and alleyways and find me a man who bit a dog! If you do that we would put the piece in the front page."

—Translated by Kamal Abdel-Malek

10.

The Trip to America (1930)

MUHAMMAD LABIB AL-BATANUNI was a noted Egyptian agriculturist who visited the United States in 1927 upon the invitation of an American agricultural institution to participate in an international conference on the soil studies. He published his account of life in America first in the Egyptian daily *al-Ahram,* and then he collected the installments in a book that he published in 1935 under the title, *The Trip to America.* The book is illustrated throughout with maps and pictures of scenes from America. Some of the topics in the book are: New York City; the Stock Exchange; American men, their mentality and their ways; American women, their work, their rush to marry and their rush to ask for divorce; American universities; American hotels; The Ku Klux Klan; the Masons, and so on.

The weather in New York City is not good at all for one's health. In summer, it is too hot and too humid to the extent that it makes one totally frazzled; it is also too cold in winter to the extent that one's blood almost freezes in one's veins . . . as for its air, it is polluted by the exhaust from the hundreds of thousands of cars that are interminably, day and night, running about the city. And because it is so hot in New York, you often see shops that sell juices such as orange and pineapple; you also see this in groceries, restaurants, and even pharmacies.

I wonder if it is the heat that causes Americans to chew gum all the time, even when walking in the street; you see men, women, and children chewing gum and carelessly spitting in public!

At any rate what I am noting here about this city is no more than a tourist's observations. It is what I saw; it pales in comparison to what I have not seen. One can view many things in a hurry and not know exactly which to write about and which to ignore. As the classical Arab poet puts it:

> Many were the gazelles that passed by the hunter
> But he was unable to decide which to catch.

What may I write about a city such as New York in which it seems all the 48 states that formed the United States are amalgamated in one and joined to New York's visitors and foreign businessmen? What may I write about New York's psychological, social, industrial, commercial, and economic aspects when I stayed in it for only a short time?

This account of New York City is at least more than the one sentence that all the geography books in Egypt say about it: "And New York is a city famous for its Brooklyn Bridge."

—Translated by Kamal Abdel-Malek

11.

The Flying Sphinx [in America] (1946?)

MAHMUD TAYMUR (1894–1973) was one of the most prominent
short story writers in Egypt. Several of his short story collections have
been translated into French, German, Italian, English, and Russian.
He also wrote novels, such as *The Call of the Unknown,* plays, and a
number of important studies on modern Arabic literature. In the late
1940s, he visited the United States and published his account in *The
Flying Sphinx [in America]*.

We quickly exited the aircraft, crossing through a walkway, which like
the green palms of an orchard afforded us shade and shelter. We
reached the main airport building and it consisted of a series of rooms and
passageways distinctly American in their naive conception of beauty and
good design. We ended up in a cramped room only to find ourselves waiting at the end of a long line. Groups of travelers, absorbed in thought, filed
into narrow columns up against the walls of the room. The delay was so
long that we were forced to find refuge in that old delightful weapon of
idle chattering, which distracted us from the tedium of waiting.

Every now and then, one of the airport employees, a short American,
would walk in dignified steps through the groups of travelers, unwilling to
catch the gaze of anyone. No sooner did he disappear into a space behind
the door than he would return to our room, utterly unconcerned with our
affairs. Every time he would emerge, our entreating eyes would fix upon
his face. His incessant comings and goings aroused our wonder and irrita-
tion. Is he really too busy for us? Some petty officials would resort to these
empty displays of self-importance just to fill the needs of their egos.

Finally, a voice called out our names . . .

We presented ourselves to a tall young doctor with a beaming face, who
cheered us up with a welcoming smile and offered us respite from the tedium of question and inquiry. The rest of the customs proceedings went

on smoothly, I even started to reconsider my negative impressions of the American customs and thought to myself that it was remarkable, good, and important.

We left the customs office followed by some black porters carrying our luggage, and got into a taxi.

I felt a sudden pang of the excitement and anxiety, much like a child who embarks on some unknown journey. A burning sense of curiosity and interest ignited in me. I glanced in every direction, in fear of missing out on anything.

America is a vast tract of earth through which lengthy highways run, with blackened asphalt, on which speeding automobiles steal across. We experienced going up and down through enormous bridges, as if we were flung back and forth from bridge to bridge. What kind of bridges were these? Were they suspended over water, or built on the ground? I could not tell.

We started to enter the built-up areas. The deeper we went into the urban jungle, the higher the buildings and the thicker the concrete foliage. We saw boulevards swarming with pedestrians. Our car slowed its pace, until we found ourselves in the midst of skyscrapers. I imagined that I was aboard a ship sailing through a great gulf walled on both sides by gigantic mountains.

It is indeed a strange feeling that envelops a human being when he passes in between these soaring towers. A man feels that he has been rendered insignificant in front of these intimidating constructions. In one instant the power and greatness of America becomes manifest. In their magnificence, these tall skyscrapers expose the obvious (and not so obvious) truths about America: its civilization, wealth, genius, dynamism, and ambition. These skyscrapers are like the pyramids of Egypt. The sight of which captures the essence of a grand culture; they immediately conjure up the minute details of a civilization and its secrets. For example, you know at once that the grave was paramount in ancient Egypt: a repository of knowledge, art, and the rule of law. How valuable these dumb stones are in articulating the mysteries of history and culture!

Here these towering edifices climb toward the sky and never cease to climb. They are eloquent in expressing the inherent inferiority complex in the American psyche, which prompts this young rising nation that has been blessed with resources, knowledge, and an undisputed position among nations, to cry out to the world: "Look at me, I am the greatest one of all!"

—Translated by Shakib Alireza

12.

America Under the Microscope (1954)

ZAKI KHALID was a noted Egyptian bacteriologist who worked for the Egyptian Ministry of Health. He was also a fellow of the London Lister Institute. In 1952, he was invited by the U.S. State Department to visit medical research institutions in the United States and to meet with his American counterparts in the field of bacteriology. He stayed four months and visited several American cities such as Washington, D.C., New York, Chicago, and Atlanta. Some of the topics covered in his book are: the Cinerama, forensic medicine in America, American cuisine, amazing American medical inventions, spare parts for the human body, American personalities, the American economy, and his opinion of Americans.

From the moment I returned to Egypt after my trip to America, everyone asked me time and again about my opinion of the Americans and how I found life among them. The reason behind this curiosity has perhaps to do with our tendency in Egypt to describe anything that is strange or abnormal as "American." Most probably we have formed this opinion of America because it is so far away from us and because most of our information about it derives not from American but European sources, and these are not always fair.

Even though mine was an official visit to the United States based on an invitation from its government, as I have mentioned earlier, I was given total freedom to choose which city to visit and which people I wished to meet. I managed to make trips all over America from coast to coast, but of course it was not possible for me to visit every single state. I have however met Americans from all walks of life and in this way I can certainly give a good account about them and answer some of the questions posed to me about life in America.

First, in America one is given the opportunity to reach the top. Even if you start from scratch, you can become a millionaire, an ambassador, or even the president of the republic. The only condition you have to satisfy is to work hard and on your own, no one will help you. It is your own task and you alone will have to carry it out.

Second, there are no social classes in America, neither aristocracy nor anything else. While it is true that the early immigrants to the United States tried to create an aristocracy and managed to set up parochial schools, private clubs, even neighborhoods for their class alone, these attempts did not continue for long and in fact were discontinued due to the fierce objections from the overwhelming majority. Now the only thing that distinguishes you in America is "success." This success is measured by what you have managed to acquire in terms of wealth or prestige for literary or scientific achievements. It is no wonder then to see people in America working and working in order to achieve and accumulate more wealth than others do and to outdo them. Who among us does not wish to distinguish himself and make money? Besides, making money is the only way to acquire all these commodities and luxuries to furnish your home or your office, and to benefit yourself and your family.

Some people fault Americans for their love of money and their desire to make it. But for God's sake tell me where is this person who does not love making money? In Europe and elsewhere we see the aristocrats and the rulers burdening millions of people with pressure and taxes in order to make money out of them. In America, however, there is no aristocracy to suck the blood of the common people. Even the millionaire in America works in order to show his compatriots that he is capable of producing something.

The fact is, as I saw it in America, you will not be judged by *how much* money or prestige you acquired but *how* you acquired it. For example, I noticed that Americans objected to collecting money for the sake of education (and it is indeed a very honorable cause) through a lottery and preferred direct donations instead.

Compare these American ways with what is going on in Europe: In France, for example, there is a custom of paying the groom a dowry. The bigger the dowry the more attractive the whole thing is (to the groom). In fact, the groom may even invest the dowry money and live off the interest! In America, on the other hand, you will find that however great the wealth of the wife's parents, the young couple would live on the husband's salary since he would consider it humiliating to live off his father-in-law's wealth.

Another admirable thing about the American is that when he earns a sum of money, however small it may be, he would try to invest it in one

way or another. And if he lost his money, the American would not feel like
he lost part of himself and would not mope around telling sad stories to
everyone he met. On the contrary, he would tend to conceal his personal
misfortune so that it might not be interpreted as a failure in his work. Instead of bemoaning his luck, he would start again to remedy the situation
and learn from his mistakes. The European on the other hand, would fret
and make a big fuss about the whole matter and would certainly be extremely happy to make money without exerting any effort. After the great
depression in America in the 1930s, a Parisian newspaper wrote that if the
same depression had taken place in France it would have reached cata-
strophic proportions: sheer terror everywhere, suicides, massive street
demonstrations, strikes, government collapse, and all this would have taken
place the same day. But in America everything was calm. The victims of
this depression sat down to assess the damage and to think over solutions
and plan for their future. The Parisian newspaper concluded that indeed
France and America were very different worlds, cultures, and *mentalités.*

All this may be valid, but I must state my objection to the American's
tendency to continue to strive to accumulate more money even after his
retirement. The temptation and the strong desire to accumulate wealth is
understandable, I must admit. But the body and the soul have needs and
these needs ought to be met in the right stage in one's life. . . . When you
look at the residents of New York City running about in the streets and
rushing to work you think they are all in a backbreaking race of sorts.

—Translated by Kamal Abdel-Malek

13.

My Days in America (1955)

ZAKI NAJIB MAHMUD was a prominent Egyptian scholar and a professor of philosophy at the University of Cairo. He wrote many books on the history of Western and Islamic philosophy and published widely in Arabic newspapers opinion pieces characterized by austere rationalism. From 1953 to 1954, he was a visiting professor at Columbia University and the University of Western Illinois. He visited several American cities such as Washington, D.C., New York, Los Angeles, San Francisco, and Seattle, and recorded glimpses of his sojourn in his 1955 *My Days in America*.

Wednesday, September 16, 1953 (on the plane)

I departed Cairo today at noon. I found myself seated beside a young man whom I thought to be an Iraqi. I found out quickly, however, that he was actually from Nicaragua. He was his country's general consul to the Trans-Jordan and Israel. He spoke in halting fragmented Arabic. As soon as we ascended above the wispy clouds, scattered against the yellow background that was the Western Desert, the flight attendant began serving pieces of peppermint. Forty minutes later, we heard over the speaker, "We are now above the city of Alexandria." So, I looked out the window to find that "Alexandria" appeared to be nothing more than some lines as fine as those drawn with a pencil on a piece of paper. As I reminisced about the family and friends I knew there, I thought, "If a vast city can be transformed into thin lines, what order of magnifier will allow me to see the people?" One is inclined, in cases like this, to deem oneself insignificant. Indeed, if a little altitude renders humans invisible, how would they appear to spectators from distant orbits and other universes? The error in this perception, of course, lies in overlooking the fact that the plane, which enables man to ascend, is in fact of his making, a creation of his leaping intellect, ambition, and imagination. The first line that ought to be written in the Book of Our Revolution, and read a thousand times each day, is that we must decide for ourselves to believe in mankind's power and omnipotence, and erase from our minds the unceasing and overpowering delusion that man is a weak and insignificant creature.

As we left the yellowness of sand to fly over the blueness of water, I bid my homeland farewell. We stopped in Athens, Rome, Zurich, Paris, and Shannon, Ireland. From there we crossed the Atlantic Ocean. The flight attendant explained to us how lifejackets are worn, should the plane be forced to make an emergency landing on water.

An American priest boarded the plane in Paris. He sat next to me. He was tall and heavyset, and he was beardless. Nothing in his appearance indicated he was a man of religion, except his black vest. He was the first American I conversed with on my journey to America. I embarked on this journey with the intention of observing the American people closely. My judgments would be based solely upon what I would see and hear. Since a nation is but the sum of its individuals, my personal opinion of the Americans would be formed through my encounters and dialogues with individuals. Therefore, I would listen carefully to every conversation, and interpret my interlocutor's every facial expression.

This American priest exuded kindness from the very first moment. He was willing to offer me any assistance I might require. After I thanked him for the cup of coffee he had taken from the flight attendant and given to me, we engaged in conversation. I asked him if he had been to Egypt. He replied, "No, the farthest I have traveled is Rome. I have crossed the ocean twice." When he found out I was Egyptian, he asked, "What are the facts about the situation between you and the English?" He quickly added, "Pardon me! I believe your problem is with the French, not the English." I corrected his oversight and explained to him that our main problem was indeed with the English. He then asked me, "So, you are dominated by Britain and you do not want her to rule you. Is that the situation?" I smiled and said, "The issue is neither domination nor rule. Egypt is an independent, free country. The point of contention is the presence of British military forces on our soil, in the region of the Suez Canal. We wish to expel those forces." Suddenly, he asked me about the number of Catholics in Egypt. As we talked, I was surprised by how his obvious ignorance of Egypt had given way to abundant knowledge and profound understanding, just from our conversation and my explanations. Had he not been so preoccupied by Catholicism, to the extent of relating every subject of discussion to it, he would have made a refined and knowledgeable man.

He offered me a cigarette, but I respectfully declined because I do not smoke. He replied, "I do not smoke cigarettes either except on trips like these. I usually smoke only cigars." When he found out that I am a specialist in philosophy, he asked me about existentialism and rational positivism, and how the two related to Catholicism. So, I explained to him my point of view on existentialism and rational positivism, but I refused to relate them to religion, leaving him to talk about this side of the issue as much as he pleased, for it preoccupies him more than it preoccupies me, and concerns him more than it concerns me.

The conversation then led us to Communism, which he proceeded to condemn with amazing enthusiasm. He was afire with a rage one would not expect from a man of religion, whose nature should be one of peace and calmness. He said, as if giving a speech to a great crowd before him even though he was only talking to one person aboard a plane cruising high above the ocean through the darkness of night, "I have declared many times in my church that I am willing to collect tithes and give the money to anyone who desires to embrace Communism and go to Russia. Once he entered Russia he would have the right to embrace the Communism he so desired. But if the gates to Russia were shut in his face and he returned with nothing but his own soiled sandals, why would he then believe in a notion whose very proponents refuse to open their gates for him to join them?"

The cabin lights were shut off and the travelers reclined in their seats in an attempt to sleep. I rested my head and slept for two hours. I felt slightly chilly, so I covered myself with the small blanket that had been on the seat. Then I slept again for about an hour. The travelers were sleeping or at least seemed as if they were. I looked out at the ocean. Of course, I saw nothing, for the altitude was so great. I did, however see a silvery, shimmering sky. There might have been a full moon that night, and the moonlight could have reflected off the clouds beneath us, thus creating that air of silver. I could feel myself breathing. I am not sure if it was a normal consequence of the altitude or solely a personal phenomenon.

I continued to gaze through the window at the silver atmosphere. I thought to myself, "There can be worlds of difference between one person and another. Compare yourself now to Columbus crossing this same ocean, and you will realize the tremendous difference that exists between a creative, innovative individual, and those who follow. . . ." We in Egypt are easily confused. We do not realize the great difference between him who researches, innovates, and spreads the results, and he who comes after that to read those results, to study and understand them. We say to ourselves, "Among them there are scientists, and among us there are as well. There is no difference between one people and another, nor is there a difference between East and West." But that difference, my friend, is like the difference between me and Columbus in crossing the ocean. He crossed as a daring adventurer, a creative and shrewd pioneer. I, on the other hand, crossed it after him, following his path, no adventure, no daring, no creativity, and no thought.

Thursday, September 17, 1953

Morning washed over us after we had spent close to 15 minutes in the darkness of night because we were heading westward, with the sun; it was as if we were in a race and did not want the sun to catch us, though it did eventually. As the day dawned I looked to find that we were flying over thick clouds, a panoramic and indeed beautiful spectacle. It seemed as if the clouds underneath us had turned into mountains of soapy foam, or billowing accumulations of white smoke.

I started talking again with the priest next to me. As soon as we began, he opened the subject of Catholicism. He urged me to go and meet the Catholic priest at my destination, the town of Columbia in the state of South Carolina. He went on some more, reassuring himself that he had understood my opinions on the philosophies of existentialism and rational positivism and that religion was impervious to their dangers. He told me at the end, "You will find all Americans to be like me. You can have with them highly elevated, intellectual conversations, like the one we had, but when you utter the words 'rational positivism,' they will ask you in ignorance, 'How tall is this building, rational positivism?'" So, I informed him that, to the contrary, the leaders of this intellectual, philosophical movement are in fact in America. We merely follow their footsteps and hardly ever come up with something new.

The plane landed in Gander, Canada. The weather was cold and damp. An official then boarded the plane to check that we had certificates of immunization against smallpox. All the passengers had health certificates except one man, a diplomat from Mexico. We all left the plane but he was ordered not to leave his place. We remained at the airport lounge for a short while. There I saw a machine that polishes shoes. You insert two cents and it starts to spin. You then put your shoe in a special place where it will be polished. Then you put in another place for the machine to make it shiny.

We then proceeded on our flight from Gander to Boston and my neighborly priest resumed his dialogue with me. He asked me if I had heard Father Sheen's announcements on television. I told him I had not, nor had I even heard of him. He said to me, "You will not reside in the States for one week without hearing him everywhere, for he is widely distinguished on both radio and television." He then described to me how the man is a charismatic preacher who attracts listeners and spectators with his looks, gestures, sound, and voice. One of the interesting things he told me about Father Sheen, is that he once performed an experiment in broadcasting, where he broadcast his program at the same time as a popular comedy show. Through this experiment Father Sheen wanted to find out which would attract people's attention more: a preacher uttering words of religious wisdom, or a comedian joking around and laughing. Triumph was to Father Sheen. Most people watched his program, proving that Americans were religious and respected their faith and its icons.

We arrived at the New York airport after 33 hours of flying. My watch was still set to Cairo time, eight o'clock. So, I set it backward six hours so that it was on New York time. I was received by a lady who had a list given to her by the State Department of foreigners expected to arrive that day. I quickly found out that she was a member of a voluntary association whose purpose was to receive foreign scholars and students and help them adjust to their new country, so that they would not feel lost or alienated. One might be inclined to think that this would be the only association committed to this humanitarian task, for indeed one association seems more than enough for this matter. I was surprised, however, when the lady gave me a list of the addresses of 34 voluntary associations, all of which were committed to guiding foreign visitors.

I walked out of customs and stood waiting for the public shuttle from the airport to the city. A police officer came up to me and greeted me saying, "You must be glad to be back home. I have the same feeling when I come back after a long leave." I replied, "I am indeed glad to have arrived here, but I am really a visitor, not an American." The police officer then went on to tell me, in a very kind and friendly manner, how fraternity and friendliness should dictate peoples' behavior, regardless of their origins or homelands. He then asked me curiously, "Why do wars emerge between one people and another, like the Korean War, for instance? Wouldn't every man wish to live among his people?" Among other things, he also said that he was Italian. At first I did not understand what he meant. He clearly meant he was of Italian origin, but I could not grasp why his European origin would be among the first things this American would tell me about himself. By then the car had arrived and the police officer helped me carry my luggage. He asked the driver to take care of me and described to him the shortest way to my hotel.

I had talked so far with three people, the priest on the plane, the volunteer at the airport, and this policeman. If this was a sample of the nation I had come to visit, it must be a friendly, generous, good-hearted, and helpful nation.

Friday, September 18, 1953

I woke up early and went to see the streets of New York in the tranquillity of morning. I wandered around, taking my time, gazing at this, touching that, standing at an intersection. When working hours began, I went to John Whitney's institution in that grand building at Rockefeller Square, the institution that had generously granted me a scholarship to stay in America for an academic year and lecture in two of its universities, the University of South Carolina in Columbia for the first half of the year, and the State College in Washington State for the second. Miss L., a 25-year-old woman, or perhaps a little older, with a pleasant face and beautiful features received me. She was elegant yet modestly dressed, and her appearance painted her as a cultured, demure person. She received me very warmly, and gave me the first portion of my grant. She then invited me to have lunch with the president of the institution, Dr. W.

During the few minutes Miss L. took while helping me obtain my salary from the cashier on the ground floor of the building, she informed me that John Whitney, the owner of the institution and the donor of the grant, was slightly over 40, and that he had won his enormous fortune in a horse race. His name was mentioned whenever there was a nationwide horse race. Therefore, he wanted to change his life in order to establish his fame in other areas. So, he engaged in numerous business enterprises—one of the most important of which is packaging frozen food—and has now reached the apex of fame in the field of commerce. I then remembered that when I was talking to the priest on the plane, I had told him I was a visiting professor with a grant made possible by John Whitney, the man of millions. The priest's reply was "Is he Whitney, the race man?" I asked, "What race? I doubt it, for all I know about this man is that he is a patron of scholarship and scholars."

I left Miss L. to return to the institution's office at lunch. Before walking the city streets, I sat on a nearby bench. I spread the map before me to see where I could go. I decided to visit three places that morning: the Empire State building, which was the tallest building in the world; the New York Public Library; and the United Nations building. In truth, it doesn't take one long to become accustomed to New York's skyscrapers, as if one had been raised there. They are the same as those seen in pictures and on screens, and one quickly ceases to be amazed.

I entered the Public Library to find it beyond belief in elegance, grandeur, cleanliness, and good taste. On its gate I saw an advertisement for an exhibit of Emerson's papers, so I made them the object of my visit. I stood in the exhibition room looking at the pages of Emerson's handwriting in glass cases. I read a few of his letters and found his handwriting extremely clear. I was amazed to be able to read the personal letters of a great literary figure such as Emerson as if he were a common man like the rest of us with small and trivial matters in his life. I sat on a chair in one of the library halls. I looked at the walls, the ceiling and the floor and an unfortunate image of the Public Library at Bab el-Khalq in Cairo came to mind. It made me shudder with alarm, for I had forgotten that the difference between one people and another can reach such a great extent. Indeed, comparing America to my country is unfair, for I am comparing one of the richest nations on earth with a nation that is among the world's poorest. That is a fact. What amazes me, however, is that we sometimes volunteer to show foreigners around our Public Library at Bab el-Khalq, as if it were a place of which we were very proud.

I looked at the people in the streets but did not find the signs of hurried busyness that I had expected. I had read the account of an Egyptian writer who had visited New York and wrote that whenever he would ask someone on the street a question they would apologetically refuse to answer, or would not even apologize, for everyone seemed to him to have been running and had no time to stop and answer any questions. I did not witness any of that. These people were like any others, with big hearts. You could ask any one of them a question and they would stop and tolerate your poor, broken English and try to understand what you were saying and then guide you to the best of their ability.

I had lunch with Dr. W. and Miss L. from the John Whitney Institute. At the table, our conversation mostly revolved around a question Dr. W. had asked, "What do Egyptians think of Americans?" I answered him honestly, "The Egyptians' opinion of Americans is unfortunately drawn from the cinema. The American is for them, as for the rest of the world, a rich man, with little culture and strange whims." I then added that an estimation of American civilization is a rather problematic proposition. "Some people elevate it to great regard, and others disparage it." Dr. W. said, "The blame here lies on those who use terms without considering their precise meanings. What exactly does the term 'American Civilization' mean? Who is an 'American' in the first place? And what is the definition of 'civilization'? Do you think all Americans are alike? You will soon be going to the South, and you will see a different strain of people, a different lifestyle, and a point of view that differs greatly from what you see here in New York, or from what you might see in the Midwest or on the West Coast. Which of these is the 'American'? Moreover, what exactly do they mean by 'American civilization'?" W. continued in this manner. I found him in complete agreement with my method of thinking, for I am one who advocates clarifying the jargon that is used so randomly in conversation.

I told him, "Those who speak of 'American civilization' most probably have in mind a civilization based on science alone, lacking the humanitarian side of faith, art, and so on." Miss L. interjected, "That is
unfortunately a common opinion of us all over the world. Therefore, you
will find the political authorities here are overly concerned with the lib-
eral arts in education."

She asked me about our scientists' opinion of American scientific
achievements. I answered honestly again, "Scientists back home tend to
wrongly accuse American science of superficiality. For instance, a psychol-
ogist back in Egypt once told me that his American counterparts are su-
perficial, even though he himself could only be found reading American
references." Miss L. asked, "How then do you explain this accusation?" I
replied, "Perhaps it is a relative issue. Americans produce more than others.
It is impossible for all their products to be of high quality. Thus, the impression one gets is that little is of high quality and the majority is of in-
ferior quality, even though the amount of high-quality product in America
is still greater than that of any other country." Dr. W. liked my explanation,
and said, "In agreement with what you have just said, I would like to add
the following: Americans are richer than others are. The outcome is that
many of them, of different social statures, can afford to leave the country
and visit other countries. Therefore, if we presume that only one out of
every five Americans visiting foreign countries is from the intelligentsia,
the impression other peoples might come away with is that only a minority of Americans are refined, while the majority are unrefined, uncultured,
and churlish. And the case in other countries, such as England for example, is that only the very elite can afford to travel abroad. Thus, the impression is that the English are a refined people."

I went that night to the Cinerama, which is a new kind of movie theater. The screen was a little more curved. That night's feature was not a
continuous story, but a montage of random scenes. It began with a man
proclaiming the birth of this new technology in the cinema industry. And
after exhibiting the different phases of development of the idea of filming
motion since the stone age, he began showing three-dimensional pictures.
First we saw a roller-coaster scene that overwhelmed us with the feeling
of actually descending and ascending, as if we were riding in a descending
and ascending vehicle. Then there was a scene of a castle of Edinburgh,
Scotland, with a Scottish pipe band, followed by a scene from Madrid,
Spain, with music and folk dancing and bull fighting, and finally a stroll
through the streets of the Italian city of Venice. The most beautiful specta-
cle of all was a scene from the Opera Aida at the Opera House of Rome.
After that they showed some images of America from Florida to the
Rocky Mountains. In short, they have succeeded greatly in giving shape

to pictures and depicting the third dimension. With this achievement, the cinema industry has made a tremendous new leap. Henceforth, God has destined these people to lead, and us to follow. He has destined them to produce, and us to consume. He has destined us to deceive ourselves that they have their civilization and we have ours, that their civilization is materialistic while ours is spiritual.

Saturday, September 19, 1953

I walked along Broadway on my very first evening. It seemed as if I were cutting my way through a sea of human torsos. Most people seemed aimless. I even heard a man stop his companions and ask them, "So, where are we going? Or must we walk the streets aimlessly?" I thought to myself, "This is so very inconsistent with what I had generally heard in Egypt about the people of America, and about New York in particular." For I had been told that I was going to find a nation that does not cease to work even for a moment, and never has any free time.

On my way I arrived at a magnificent building called Radio City before which stood a line of people waiting to enter. So, I stood in line, and when my turn came, I entered. What greatness surrounded me, on the floor, on the walls, and on the ceiling! Superb carpets and paint, and beautiful ornamentation, and lights that overwhelm sight and leave one's soul in awe. What I found rather strange is how little it cost to enter this most elegant building. There I saw a new movie, *Roman Holiday*, a musical. Watching this movie in itself was worth many times the amount I had paid. One of the strangest scenes was the sight of a man with a bag that seemed to contain another man! The small bag opened to actually let out a man, even though it was too small to even contain a kitten. The man emerges from the bag and amazes the spectators with his great ability to imitate the sounds of a foxhunt. You could hear him imitating a multitude of sounds all at once: the sound of foxes, dogs, horses, and the hunters. . . .

Sunday, September 20, 1953

The Sunday *New York Times* newspaper is a marvel that would amaze you. It is a huge load, equal to 30 or 40 *al-Ahram* newspapers. It is a newspaper that deserves admiration. If the press is the mirror that reflects public opinion, and if the *New York Times* is the mirror of American public opinion, then it is a public opinion that has been elevated to a very high level of sedateness, gravity, emotional restraint, and objectivity. You can read it and not find one article that contains nonsense, boring repetition, or empty droning. Every article is solid opinion, superbly crafted, whose fragments are completely coherent. In these articles you will find originality. One can be satisfied with its weekly political summary alone, which summarizes that week's political happenings around the world.

I went to see what New York was like on Sundays. I did not find it as quiet as London is on Sundays. In the streets there was motion, even though it was mild. I went to take the underground metro without having any particular intention aside from familiarizing myself with it. There I was stunned by what a disgrace it was to this great city, in which all was elegant and grandiose like a silent tongue challenging the whole world to produce something of the same high quality. This underground metro, however, was a blight on one great book. It is old, filthy, vibrates when it moves, and bears many signs of negligence.

Monday, September 21, 1953

I left New York by plane, heading to Columbia, South Carolina, where I was to lecture in philosophy for the first half of the year. I stopped briefly in Washington, D.C. where I met Dr. A. I discussed with her what was actually expected of me during my visit. I also quickly visited my friends at the office of delegations and the Egyptian embassy. I resumed my flight to Columbia and arrived at dusk. Dean N. and Dr. S., two of the most respected men of the university, were there to receive me. I was amazed, and even puzzled, when the graceful men both raced to help me with my luggage and put it in the dean's car. Then they accompanied me to the hotel in which I was to stay. In truth, I then imagined an American professor visiting Egypt, as I visited America today, and asked myself, "Would any of our professors even think of receiving him at the airport, as these two men have received me, and taking care of him until they were sure he had settled in?" For we tend to overlook these humanitarian gestures, and insist instead on babbling since the matter does not exceed babble, that Americans live in a materialistic civilization that lacks human values. While we, on the other hand, enjoy and live in a spiritual civilization.

It seems that all hotels here are similar in furniture and facilities, for the room in which I was staying bore great resemblance to my room in New York. Having seen the Bible placed on a desk in both rooms is enough resemblance. I just hope that I will not miss these small observations, for they bear profound implications. And here I am witnessing increasing evidence of the real nature of America that testifies to the piety of the American people, something I really did not expect. I wonder what an American visitor to Egypt staying at the Semiramis Hotel for instance would say if he found a Quran in every room.

After spending only a few minutes in my room, the telephone rang. The speaker on the other line was Dr. F., the professor of philosophy at the university. He was welcoming me upon my safe arrival, and suggested a meeting if I was not too tired. I welcomed his visit. Dr. F. is one of those people for whom the study of philosophy has given them a mental alertness and intellectual enlightenment evident merely in the sparkle of their eyes. Studying, from what I have witnessed in my life, leads scholars either to this kind of alertness and enlightenment or to sluggishness and stupor. Dr. F. is of the first category. He welcomed me and took me in his car to his office at the university. His office was also his library, as is the case for all professors. All four walls in the office were hidden by bookshelves. His office was the place where he worked and studied at the same time. Each professor had an office like this in which he placed his materials, books, and papers. If students were told to get in touch with their professor, they would know where to find him, for he would be settled there. Any student that wanted to see a professor could seek him out in his special place. Is it possible for me to see this and not compare it to our miserable condition in Cairo? There, all philosophy professors are packed into one room, with space for only one desk. Where can a professor (back home) sit to conduct work? Where can a professor sit without being quickly forced to return to his home as soon as he's done with lectures? Where can he sit and really be there for students to meet?

I spoke with Dr. F. about the lectures I was to deliver about Islamic philosophy, and found out that people were awaiting these lectures to generally learn things they did not know about Islam, Arabs, and the Middle East. Most professors arranged to attend these lectures. Moreover, many individuals, outside the university, requested to attend. Before my arrival, the University had announced my lectures on Arab thought, which was an incentive for many to prepare themselves for them. . . .

Wednesday, September 23, 1953

It was a bright, beautiful day, which appeared wonderfully before my eyes. I felt my heart beat in ecstasy and happiness. I rose early and looked out the window. It had a strong screen to keep out the mosquitoes. Everything outside seemed bright and vivid. I turned on the radio to listen to music, and add to the ecstasy of that morning.

Today, I delivered my first lecture on Arab philosophy. In it, I analyzed those characteristics of Arab thought that distinguish it from Western thought. I felt confident of what I was saying. Among those present was a Mrs. S. who, from the very first minute, attracted my attention. Indeed it could have even been before that, because she had come up to me before the beginning of the lecture to ask me where I would be speaking. She introduced herself sufficiently and asked me to pronounce my name so that she could pronounce it properly. She said that she and her husband, an officer at the military hospital of the air force, were planning to live in Egypt for some time. They wanted to know all there was to know about Egypt. She seemed intelligent, not to mention femininely attractive. Everything in her attire and jewelry implied refined taste. It seems that, no matter how candid the writer is, he will not be utterly candid, for I feel inclined to conceal some of my pride for being so fluent, eloquent, and intelligent in my first lecture that I captivated this lady and caused her to make Egypt her destination. . . .

Sunday, September 27, 1953

Members of the family that I was staying with went to church, and I remained by myself. I sat on the balcony, reading the local morning newspaper. There are two main newspapers in Columbia, one published in the morning, and one in the evening, as well as the massive Sunday newspaper, which is about ten times the size of *al-Ahram*.

A quick glimpse through these two local newspapers is more than enough to reveal the local tastes and social patterns. They are primarily concerned with state matters, the state of South Carolina, that is, followed by matters of the rest of the states, and then matters of the outside world.

When I was in Egypt I used to get frustrated by the tribal spirit common to our newspapers, even the more important ones. You would find that our newspapers dedicated many articles to the news of individuals, so-and-so traveled, and the other one passed away, and these people were appointed to elevated official posts in the government, and so on with such nonsense that should not occupy space in a newspaper, which should really be above these trivialities. When I found some resemblance to that in the local newspaper here, of course you would never find something like that in a mainstream newspaper such as the *New York Times,* I realized that the narrower the circle of people's interests was in a society, the more their newspapers reflect their domestic nature, becoming pseudo-bulletins. On the other hand, the wider the horizon, and the more elevated the culture, the more the newspapers weave their nets around the whole world and ignore trivial news.

From what I can see, people here almost shut their windows to the outside world. They know very little, or perhaps even less than little. In fact, they seem to be indifferent to the goings-on of distant states. Their newspapers, the morning *State* and the evening *Columbia Record,* reflect this. It is more important for newspapers here to fill their pages with pictures of brides that got engaged or married than to publish even the slightest news of the revolution in Egypt.

I sat on the balcony for the whole afternoon. The mistress of the house approached me holding food in a yellow wrapper. She told me she was going to the park to feed the worms. I gazed at her in amazement and curiosity. She said, "Yes, I feed worms. There are a number of worms in my park, to which I take food. I pity them. Years ago I used to fear them and feel disgusted by them because they will feed on my corpse after I am dead, but now I pity them. The least that can be said of them is that they are beneficial to the soil and agriculture without actually harming us. There are few things that contribute and do no harm. For that, I go every-day to the park and feed a big group of worms there." I told her, "I heard a cat's constant meow coming into my room from the back window. Is there a caged cat in the park?" She replied, "No, that is a bird who sounds like a cat. I do not feed cats and do not like them either, because they feed on birds. I have a friend whose name is so-and-so. He loves birds so much that he formed a committee the sole purpose of which is to get rid of cats, and therefore maintain and protect the bird population. The committee, however, has made it its principle not to harm cats, but to collect them into one place as much as possible. That way the cats live and so do the birds. My friend pays a dollar for each cat that joins his 'camp' of cats."

Tuesday, September 29, 1953

The owner of the house in which I was staying was a retired priest. He had spent most of his life as a preacher in Korea and China. His name was M. How wonderful this man was in his sincere goodness, modesty, and true helpfulness. He reminded me of the priest I met on the flight from Paris to New York. Am I allowed to generalize, seeing these two examples, and say that a Christian man of religion is truly a man of faith, considering his modesty and sacrifice for others? Would it be just if I said, based upon my short experiences with these two men, that a man of religion here not only believes in his faith, but lives it? Here, I almost wrote, "On the other hand, our men of religion . . ." But then I stopped myself saying, "The term men of religion does not exist in our hemisphere. Every Muslim is a man of religion. That is, every Muslim is responsible for his faith before his God . . ." At any rate, I found myself forced to make this statement, "Those who call themselves men of religion back home are those who know the pillars of our religion by heart. They study religion like mathematics or geography are studied, but they do not live it."

Dr. S., the chairman of the university's department of philosophy called me and told me he was going to arrange four meetings in his house on days he specified and invite to each meeting a group of professors for me to meet. I thanked him sincerely and warmly for his great generosity. Dr. S. is a rare example of a polite, well-mannered man. I swear to God, I have never met a man of his like. Why would he offer me so much help, giving up much and investing so much effort? I am amazed that these people are known for leading materialistic lives while we Egyptians consider ourselves spiritual. The "Americans" isn't just a meaningless term, they are human beings. If you wish to utter anything against them, keep silent until you have met individuals from amongst them so that you may find out for yourself whether the dollar really is their only motivation—as they are well-renowned for, or if they are motivated in their behavior by noble, refined, human values. Why did Dr. S. and Dean N. come to meet me at the airport, and carry my suitcases? Why would Dr. S. arrange these four get-togethers in his house for me? Why would he move a heavy chair by himself from one floor in the building to another merely to provide me with a comfortable seat? Why would he drive around with me for hours in his car, looking for a place for me to settle in? This man is an American. Was he motivated in his behavior by any material gain? Or was it because he had a big heart and noble feelings? In these memoirs of mine I write only of my direct, personal experiences and will prevent myself from accepting biased judgments passed randomly on entire nations.

If I were to be asked about the Americans, I would answer within the limits of my own experience. I would say, without hesitating, that they are characterized by friendliness and hospitality. It is impossible for one of them to sit at my table in a cafeteria without greeting me and starting a conversation. If our conversation stopped it would be because I would have stopped talking, not him.

—Translated by Tarek Masoud and Ammar Fakeeh

14.

The Land of Magic (1962)

SHAFIQ JABRI, a Syrian academic and author, visited the United States in 1953 upon an invitation from the U.S. government. At the time of this invitation he was the dean of the faculty of arts at the University of Damascus. During his stay in the United States he participated in a conference on Islamic culture sponsored by Princeton University. He published his impressions about American life in his 1962 *The Land of Magic*. The book is divided into chapters each bearing the name of an American city the author visited.

I was destined to visit America twice: the first time in 1953 and the second time in 1956. I traversed the country from east to west, and from north to south. I enjoyed seeing its many natural sites, and visiting its universities. On these visits I became acquainted with some traits that are peculiar to the American people. I learned certain characteristics about their thought processes, group gatherings, and their work. I was also acquainted with their group efforts in fending off the destructive forces of nature, after they fought off the Indians. Every day I would write down my observations about these American characteristics until I published this book that I entitled: *Land of Magic*. In some of its chapters I explain the reason for this title. If the dignified reader is able to see the faults of the book and understand the impressions that these trips made on me, the impressions that I expressed in a spontaneous and an unbiased fashion, then I will have accomplished my goal.

America's Fast-Paced, "Boiled" Life

I have friends from Syria and Lebanon who work at the radio station "The Voice of America." One day a group of them invited me to lunch at a restaurant in the radio station. So, I went with them to this self-serve restaurant, which is called a "cafeteria." In the cafeteria I saw men and women standing in a line until they reached the area where the food was displayed. There each one of them picked the different type of food they wanted to eat. They then carried the food on their trays to their seats. My friends suggested that I sit and not burden myself with choosing food. So I sat and after a few minutes they returned with their trays and I apologized because I could not digest American cooking.

During the conversation I unintentionally let my gaze rest on the different kinds of food such as boiled eggs, boiled potatoes, and boiled vegetables. I then shared with my friends my opinion about American life. I said to them, "There is a striking similarity between your food and your lives. As I see it, your food is all boiled and so is your life. You no sooner finish eating than you have to excuse yourselves to go back to work." With that they gave me directions to exit the radio station, so I left them and went to an Arabic restaurant called, Baghdad.

At the table I carried on and on about my dislike of this fast-paced American life. I object to this sort of lifestyle because it tires the mind and thought, until a human becomes a machine. From morning until noon he works, eating in a hurry, and then he returns to work. As soon as he leaves his work, he hurries to eat dinner in some restaurant. Once he finishes dinner, he goes to the movies or sleeps. There is no free time to converse with friends, or spend time alone with the family. It is as if life is all work, as if the body doesn't have any rights, and as if the soul doesn't have a chance for enjoyment. Conversations are mostly about material things. They talk in numbers and dollars. To Americans, the world is all buying and selling, winning and losing, taking and giving. There are no anecdotes to lighten the heart, no jokes for the enjoyment of the soul. This is life in America, with the exception of Saturday and Sunday nights. On these nights, each person gets as much pleasure as he can.

One of my friends said to me, "But if you ask the Americans their opinion about this lifestyle you will find that they are happy and satisfied with it." I replied, "I am not surprised. I know some peasants in my country that I've associated with for a long time. Some of them depart at sunrise to the grazing fields with four loaves of bread and a few olives. Then they return · at night and have a dinner that consists of bread and potatoes, or olives, or onions, or broken wheat. The peasant goes to sleep (at the same time the chickens do) right after he finishes dinner. He wakes up at dawn and is satisfied and happy with his life, because he doesn't know any other. He has not experienced any other type of life. This applies to Americans as well. They are satisfied with their lifestyle, but if they tried a different kind of life, one with more enjoyment and happiness, they would change their minds about their tiresome life.

One time I ate in a restaurant whose owners were from a village in Palestine. At one of the tables I saw four American men and four American women. They drank a lot of wine, ate a lot of meat, and spoke a lot. The owner of the restaurant, Aisha, brought in two musical instruments, the *daff* and the *darabukka*. She alternated playing each of them. Abraham, a young American man, originally from Palestine, got up and danced the *debka,* to the beat of the music. I took this opportunity to observe the effect of this on the Americans. As soon as the men and women saw the dance and heard the music, they got up and went to the middle of the restaurant and started dancing in a way I cannot describe. Among them was a beautiful woman who had a nice body. She was very excited with this enjoyment and happiness. Once the music died down, everyone went his own way.

To me, this incident showed how suffocated the Americans are in their environment. Any fresh air that they find, they breathe it in quickly. The beautiful lady in the restaurant who let loose was expressing her entrapment. The Americans are satisfied with their lives because they don't know any other. If they became familiar with another lifestyle that has the music of the *daff* and the dancing of the *debka,* they would ask God to spare them from their boiled life, which they spend on the run.

The American Mentality

I don't want to fool anyone by claiming that I know everything about the American mentality. This would require many years of study. In order to learn about the American mentality, one has to study the history of America and its geography. It is imperative to understand the origins of the nations that colonized it from the outset. It is also important to study the conditions of its universities and schools, governmental laws, and conditions of the social classes in each of its states. One must also mingle with these social classes to better understand the American mentality. To accomplish all these things takes a long time.

When I speak of the American mentality, I speak of only a small, generalized area. My impressions, which came to me with the speed of lightning, are only what can be gained from a trip. Some of these impressions have a portion of truth, but it is a small portion at any rate.

I entered a bookstore in Washington to buy a book on philology written by two professors from Harvard, one of the best American universities. While there, I found a book about grammar, discourse, and composition. The author is an assistant professor at New York University (NYU). I bought the book and started examining it. From the pages of the book, an aspect of the American mentality unfolded before me.

The book contained ten chapters. If we look at the content of every chapter, we find that each contains the basics of the subject without any details or complications. For each of these subjects there is a simple example so that the student can memorize the definition and the example with little effort. If you look at the examples and exercises in the book, you find that they relate closely to the American senses. A few of the examples mention vitamins. Vitamins play a big role in America. You find unusual body strength in young Americans and their children. This strength is due to two factors: their food intake and their participation in sports.

All the chapters in this book follow the same pattern of simplicity and ease. The last chapter is dedicated to references and indexes. When the student finishes reading the book, he will have a rudimentary knowledge of what he needs to know to form phrases and use references for research. This is an example of some of the characteristics of the American mentality. The Americans don't have time or patience. They want to learn as much as possible in the shortest amount of time. They want to reach the core of a subject quickly. The author crammed subjects related to grammar, discourse, and composition into this book. Had a separate book for each of these subjects been written, the reader would have been lost.

Americans are pragmatists, and time is essential to them. Instead of wasting time on details, Americans prefer to jump into the heart of the matter. Therefore, their teachers prepare knowledge for them in the same fashion a pharmacist prepares easy-to-swallow pills for patients. The students have many libraries and plenty of references, yet they have no patience. For example, when I visited one of the universities, I found the professor had prepared notes for his lecture. Five minutes into his lecture one of the students asked him a question, so the professor put aside his notes and started answering the question. When he finished answering the question, another student asked him a question and so on, one question after another until the end of the lecture. The professor's notes remained unread.

American students have no patience for abstract concepts. They want to obtain practical knowledge as soon as possible. As I see it, this narrows the thinking of American students, because they depend more on what the teachers say, than on their own thinking.

Give me as much as possible with the least amount of effort, this is part of the American mentality. I will never forget a conversation I had with a young American military officer. He said to me, "Tell me about the conditions in your country: the food, the drink, the clothes, and business." This officer wanted to know everything about Syria in one evening.

One finds a large disparity between the American and European mentality. I compared two books; one dealing with the history of the English language, and one with the French language. While the French author gives a prologue on the background of the subject, delving into the disciplines of sociology and psychology, the American author delves right into how the words are born, how they live and die, without prologues or elaboration, which the American mind does not have the capacity for.

America in Books

Coming back from a small town on the outskirts of Washington, where one of my American friends had invited me, I saw snow. It had covered the elegant houses and the quiet streets. I wanted to get away from the bustling Washington metropolis, so I stayed in the hotel and buried myself in my book for an hour.

The dean of the College of Political Science in New York said in one of his articles:

> I believe that it is not possible to achieve a good, just and happy life in any society where the economic and political authority is restricted to the hands of one person or a small group of people. I see it as President Thomas Jefferson used to see it. Humans cannot expend energy to reach happiness or to succeed in their efforts unless they are living in a democracy, even if that democracy is not complete.
>
> Finally, I believe that people of different races and beliefs can achieve those human goals if we know how to use our social skills and tradition of scientific knowledge. There will then be a day where there is no bloodshed, no hatred, no sickness, and no poverty and people will not have a destructive fear of the unknown.

I came across contradictions when I finished reading these rich ideas. On my first visit to America, I was taken by America's natural attraction and the greatness of its universities. Therefore, I did not think critically. Now I am no longer under its spell, I can look at things independently. The contradictions in America are baffling and I am not certain what the author meant when he wrote what he wrote. I am not sure whether he was trying to disparage some ethnic groups in America itself, or whether he was trying to disparage some foreign nation. Whatever he meant, he was correct. There are a lot of problems in America that he pointed out. One is the economic power, which is concentrated in a few hands. Another is the political power, which is in the hands of the Republicans or the Democrats. What prevents the masses from revolting is the extraordinary luxury of life in America, which has no equal in the whole world. Yet people still complain. They complain about taxes, Jews, blacks, and other things. These complaints notwithstanding, life in America is enjoyable, easy, and keeps people busy. An example is the average worker. No matter what his income is, at the end of the day he is able to drink whatever he wants and to eat according to his financial ability. The same is true of the middle class. The rich, on the other hand, complain only about their health.

This is what keeps Americans calm and quiet. They are not too interested in the fact that the economic and political power is concentrated in a few hands. As long as they have their necessities, such as bread, meat, and warmth, they are content. In this respect, America has reached the highest level a materialistic civilization can offer. This is the truth that should be said, but behind this statement is the beginning of the problem.

I didn't see a unified spirit in all of America. The schools and the universities that raise the young do not mold the students into one shape. The differences in character and traditions that came with the various groups who colonized America have persisted. You can therefore hear the Italian grocer singing in Italian even after living in America for 35 years. One also sees the young people from villages in Palestine and Jordan dancing the *debka* in some of Washington's restaurants even though all of them are American citizens. I still can hear a Druze with his strong accent saying, "If I became American, should I abandon my Arab origin?"

So, the Americans are not molded in one type of thought, feeling, or sentiment. If there were a crisis in the country that shook up the social norm, from either inside or outside forces, what would happen to America? After all, the social norm is people eating, sleeping, drinking, and satisfying all their needs to the fullest. Men and women in America told me if something like that happened one would find that Americans would be very patriotic, sacrificing themselves for their country. But I still have my doubts. If something akin to what I mentioned happened, would this greatness continue or would this awesome structure crumble? America is like a group of mosaic pieces, each piece standing alone. It is not like a building where each component supports the other.

—Translated by Dima Reda

15

America: Paradise and Hellfire (1982)

ADIL HAMMUDA is a well-known Egyptian journalist. He visited the
United States in early 1980s and published his account under the title
America: Paradise and Hellfire. The cover of his book shows a woman's
open mouth with glossy rounded lips and shining teeth that hold a
bullet with a picture of a cowboy on it. The topics covered in the
book include freedom in America; the mystery of the number 40 in
America; the television workout exercises, robots in America, racial
discrimination against American blacks, the "dirty Arab" stereotype in
America, the strange kind of Islam in America, American Jews, Hollywood, Native Americans, American humor and Art Buckwald.

A White House in a Black-Hearted City

New York City, America's throbbing heart, is a city without a heart. A
city that would break your heart. Three minutes after I arrived in
America, I was greeted in a very friendly manner by a New Yorker, maybe
too friendly! Outside the JFK airport I was startled when someone lay his
hand on my shoulder so harshly it hurt. I had goosebumps all over my
body. I was frightened and became more frightened when I saw a giant of
a man smiling to me, with white teeth and an artificial smile. My heart
sank. I became pale. He was tall, very tall, wearing in the middle of the hot
summer a winter fur jacket. He tucked his pants in his long socks that
reached his knees. He wore a pair of cheap plastic slippers.

I said to myself it looked like this was the end of my life. He'd stab me
in my ribs and snatch my bag and money and run away.

The giant pointed to his stomach, swaying his body, saying to me, "I'm
hungry." I tried to hold my fear from showing and I even tried to sound
friendly to him.

"How much do you need, friend?"

He moved his hand from my shoulder to his waist and said, "I want a cigarette."

Before I could reach to the packet, he beat me to it and snatched it from my pocket. He lit a cigarette and just kept the packet, saying to me, "I need three bucks!"

I felt the dollars in my pants pocket trying my best to figure out the value of the bills I was feeling. What I thought was one dollar turned out to be ten so I apologized to him for not having the right change. He just snatched the ten dollar bill from my hand and ran away, and yet to my mind this man was a kindhearted angel. Why would I call him a kindhearted angel when he had just run away with my money? It is because he just sold me my life for only ten dollars and an old packet of cigarettes. It was a very cheap price to pay for a human life in New York. Everything is expensive in New York, everything, that is, except human life.

Every day, one in every one thousand individuals in New York is assaulted, mugged, or killed. For every one hundred individuals twenty are without a job, or an opportunity to find one, and at times they are even without money. Nine individuals in every thousand belong to organized crime. Fifteen in every hundred live under subsistence level, very close to the line that separates humans from animals. If you saw New York City from the air you would not expect to see on the ground such human misery. The sight of New York city from the air looks familiar to me since I have seen it in many American movies: rectangles of cement, iron, glass, aluminum, and trees. A forest of skyscrapers . . . a city that defies heaven and kicks earth, a city that loves no one, respects no one, and submits to no one. The hearts of its residents are made of cement; their arteries are made of iron rods; their feelings are made of aluminum; their words are like flung stones. . . . It is dog-eat-dog in New York. As a stranger in New York you may be assaulted, torn apart, even killed for no reason.

. . .

For the sake of Greenwich Village, New York City ought to be forgiven for all its sins. It is a district of town made for fun and staying up all night long; it was built by Americans with the Latin Quarter of Paris in mind. It is full of bars, restaurants, and discos. Artists draw and paint everywhere: on walls, on the ground, even on clients' clothes. There you do many things while you are standing: you eat, drink, play, and make love. It is crowded everywhere as though you were in a city bus or a crowded food cooperative in a Cairo popular district (where the poor buy their subsidized groceries). Most of these restaurants and bars were once storehouses or abandoned buildings or chicken coops and were converted magically into something completely different thanks to the wallpaper, the velvet, and the dim lights.

In these restaurants and bars sheer madness and crazy fads are permitted. A patron enters with only his underwear on and is served a drink in the lid of a cooking pot; another enters dressed up like Nero, the one who burned Rome, and he is held down by two strong men who force open his mouth and pour an alcoholic drink into it, which he drinks in one gulp . . . one kind of madness draws another and is met with another. And if you behave like a sane person here in the midst of all this madness, New Yorkers suspect that you may be a cop.

Of course there is no connection whatsoever between Greenwich Village and the Latin Quarter. Here in Greenwich Village madness is inane, even silly, whereas in the Latin Quarter madness is creative and impressive; here there is no good taste, there there is every kind of good taste; here there are hooligans, there there are *artistes*.

And yet if you don't know New York, you don't know America.

—Translated by Kamal Abdel-Malek

16.

The Washington Memoirs (1986)

YUSUF AL-HASAN is a Palestinian intellectual who has lived in the United States for the last several years. In his 1986 book *The Washington Memoirs,* he gives an account of his life and work in the United States, particularly his struggle to promote the Palestinian cause. The topics covered in the book include: blacks in America, the American Right, Zionist propaganda in America, images of Arabs and Jews in the American mass media, the Amish, and Disney.

Americans do not scribble or engrave words on walls. They leave behind the memories of places and times without much fuss or sentimental attachment. For them there is no such a thing as deprived love, or romantic love with its torments. Even though they have trees all over the place, you don't see them engrave hearts pierced with Cupid's arrows and adorned with lovers' initials on their trees.

Whenever there is a clash of interests in their society, they write their demands on signs and hoist them in demonstrations. American life is basically a collection of intersecting interests and compromises. Americans are characterized by openness; they talk out loud; they don't know how to whisper. They talk as if their doors and windows were flung open.

Americans don't understand the workings of history, especially when they deal with foreign affairs. For this reason they fail to understand the logic behind events and the sequence in which they occur. "Either now or never" characterizes their attitude. When things go wrong and a crisis faces them, they rush to solve it with whatever is expedient. Outside America things are fine as long as America is not affected. If the situation abroad affects American comfort and pockets, then America interferes; it doesn't look for the reasons that led to that bad situation but seeks to punish and to "take an immediate action," just like the cowboy who lives in a world in which only the fastest to pull his gun survives. America's obliviousness [toward world crises that do not affect it] is notorious and is, in fact, un-matched in the industrialized world. America's narcissism is appalling; it would not tolerate anyone disturbing its comfortable life. The American doesn't really care about the bloodletting of hundreds of people in the Arabian Gulf, nor the ruin of the economic infrastructure and the national wealth of countries in the region. His only concern is to safeguard the flow of oil. That is all.

—Translated by Kamal Abdel-Malek

17.

America (Top Secret) (1987)

AHMAD HARIDI is an Egyptian journalist who narrates in his 1987
America (Top Secret), many humorous, but at times implausible, stories
about his life in America. Some of the topics he covers are: the Statue
of Liberty, social classes in America, the stock exchange, New York
City, illiteracy in America, violence in America, American women
and loneliness, American children, drugs, America's war machine, lobbies and interest groups in America.

Concomitant with the changes that followed when American women
entered the workplace as rivals to men was a reduction in the per-
centage of marriages, a rise in the number of divorce cases, and an excess
of men and women desiring to live together out of wedlock.

Women's ownership and management of business enterprises is not
considered something surprising, rather it has become part of the image of
the affluent American city. According to the Office of Labor Statistics, at
the end of 1986, 2.8 million American women owned business enterprises
and undertook the management by themselves. In relation to the numbers
given before 1976, the growth rate was 75 percent. At the same time, over
the same period, the number of businessmen did not exceed 6.5 million
and the growth rate was 12.1 percent.

American businesswomen owned 25 percent of the small businesses in
the year 1986. According to forecasts by the Bureau of Small Businesses, it
is expected that 50 percent of people owning businesses of this size by the
year 2000 will be married and single women.

Laura Henderson, a working woman and owner of a medical consulting
firm in Rockville, Maryland, works 16 hours a day, every day of the week.
Everything in her life, including her two-year-old child Blair, is a matter of
secondary importance, as long as her attention is devoted to her company,
which in the year 1986 amounted to a capital worth of $5.5 million.

Mary, a 37-year-old divorced mother of two kids aged 10 and 12, portrays herself, sarcastically, as "a pillar of society." She works as the manager of a hotel and has a high income. A woman of high society such as Mary is someone who considers herself one of the many ambitious American women. It is possible that she is the object of the envy of others. At the end of the week she finds herself wanting to go out to meet a man who may not be her social equal and have a fleeting relationship with him.

There is a large increase in the number of women in high management positions who take cocaine and depressants, and a few of them turn to consuming huge amounts of food. The women live a hard, harsh, and vicious life in the management seats of companies, banks, and small businesses. This pushes them to escape for some of the time and to flee the never-ceasing wheel of production into a world of chaos and lack of control in which they are totally free from all discipline and restrictions . . .

The American woman is part of the web that pervades the utilitarian American mentality, a network of relations that are controlled by two principles: money and sex. In the wealthy American cities, the ambitious woman enters the large capitalistic machine, running after riches and the highest rungs of a hierarchical society. The materialistic ambition of some American women ends with them departing from the diabolical machine with broken hearts and homes, and sick, exhausted souls, and with them drowning their wretchedness in drugs and alcohol.

The ailments of a strife-ridden and competitive society are isolation, anxiety, tension, and physical and mental exhaustion. From these ailments, capitalism benefits by saturating the market with the various types of cigarettes, tranquilizers, cocaine, and heroin used to cope with the ailments. This is all but one aspect of the perpetual running of the American machine in its wicked pursuit of profit.

The occurrence of divorce quadrupled in America between 1950 and 1982. The increase in the number of divorce cases petitioned before American judges in the year 1986 grew to more than two million cases. A steady decrease in the number of American families is to be compared to a great increase in the number of American men and women living alone, which is estimated to be close to 20.6 million.

Judgments issued by divorce courts are determined by the same principles as the ones that apply to the setting up and dissolving of commercial firms. These judgments concentrate on dividing the spoils of the marriage in accordance with the ruling of the court. Such ruling is based on who should be blamed for the failure of the marriage.

Divorce cases take a long time in the courts and the disputes do not end. The negative social and economic consequences are carried by the women and children, whose level of livelihood, according to a recent study, decreases by 73 percent after the first year of a divorce.

More than 65 million Americans carry guns in their pockets. More than half a million are automatic weapons that are small, light, easy to use, and used in wars. Individuals use these weapons on the streets of America. Two households out of every three have guns, rifles, and ammunition in their possession.

Over there, there are no detailed estimates of how many weapons are in the possession of American individuals. That is to say, a restriction limiting the sale of weapons is nonexistent, because the federal government only limits the issuing of licenses for automatic weapons.

Deadly assault weapons are made so that they carry out the desire of the American mentality to kill greater numbers of people with extraordinary speed. The total fascination and passion for bearing arms that overpowers the American individual finds its roots in the American experience in Vietnam. A madness and passion for killing increased in the extreme circles of the American Right, the racists and members of the neo-Nazi movement.

More than a billion dollars of yearly profits from New York, Houston, Los Angeles, and other American cities are from the sale of weapons and from smuggling them to Europe, Asia, the Middle East, and Latin America. America is a factory for the machines of death and destruction and an arsenal of heavy weapons. She does business in all illegal weapons, trades them and exports them across official lines to the hot spots of conflict in the world.

—Translated by Patrick Gaffney

18.

Embers and Ashes:
Memoirs of an Arab Intellectual (1988)

HISHAM SHARABI is a well-known Palestinian American scholar with expertise in Middle Eastern history and politics. Until his retirement he had been a professor of politics at Georgetown University, and he is now the director of the Center on Palestine Policy. In his somber *Embers and Ashes* he bares his soul to his readers with a searing narrative about his childhood in Palestine and his school days in the United States.

Spring finally arrived and my life turned upside down. In April, on my birthday, I received my grades for the winter semester. They were highly pleasing. With a heavy burden lifted, I felt my confidence return.

I began to frequent the library less and to spend all my evenings in the lounges with my American and Arab friends. I went out for coffee at the Greasy Spoon diner, and for beer at the bars on 55th Street.

On one of those weekday nights, I visited the Beehive, a small bar on 55th Street renowned for jazz. I joined an American friend and two young women who resided with us in the International House. After we had drunk several pitchers of beer, I felt an overwhelming urge to go to the bathroom. But embarrassment kept me from making a trip and I sat holding myself, not knowing what to do. After a little while, one of the girls got up and said while patting her abdomen, "It's the beer; it needs to find a way out."

My face turned red from embarrassment while I stood up to let her pass by me. But I took advantage of the situation and took my turn in the "men's room." In the men's room, a young American man stood beside me and turned to me after unbuttoning his pants. He wore an expression of complete bliss and said, "Now this is happiness, isn't it?"

It was my exact sentiment because I was getting rid of this heavy burden. A feeling of joy made me love the world in its entirety.

From that day on, I never hesitated to be direct when nature called.

Over the spring semester, an intimate relationship developed between me and one of my female friends in the philosophy department who was living in the International House. It did not take long to turn into a relationship of love. She was from California and had a Norwegian background; her name was Carol. We met several times outside the lecture auditorium and had lunch once or twice. . . . I told her about the lectures of Bergestraser, and she repeatedly attended them. One Saturday night I invited her to join me and my friend Rashid and his girlfriend. She accepted the invitation and that was the beginning of the relationship.

We waited for her in the lobby that night, Rashid, his girlfriend, and I. Then I saw her approaching from afar, slowly coming down the stairs. I almost didn't recognize her. Before that night, I had only seen her in old clothes that did not attract attention: a ragged vest, a wide woolen skirt, bobby socks and flats. She didn't usually use makeup. This evening, she was wearing a tight white dress, high heels, and with an expensive fur jacket draped over her shoulders. There was a small hat made of the same fur on her head and she was wearing dark red lipstick; she was truly attractive. The men who were sitting around us could not keep their eyes off her. Rashid stood up in amazement and gave her a warm welcome; I felt both anxiety and pride. As we exited the lobby, the stares followed us.

Rashid's girlfriend, who didn't trust his driving ability, especially at night, insisted that we use the subway or take a cab. Carol volunteered to drive Rashid's used Oldsmobile. I sat next to her in the front and Rashid and his girl sat in the back. That was the first time that I had gone downtown. Carol drove us on the Outer Drive, which is adjacent to the lake. The skyscrapers appeared out of the city lights, and on our right was the expanse of the lake in the darkness. As I looked at Carol gripping the steering wheel, her pretty profile became clear in the dark. She was the first American girl I fell in love with. She was 20 and I was 21. . . .

Rashid took us to a café called the Top Hat in the fanciest hotel in Chicago. We sat at a small table with a candle in the center. After the waiter lit the candle, he waited for our orders. Carol and Rashid's girl ordered sherry, Rashid ordered whiskey and I ordered a Tom Collins (it was the only cocktail name I could remember at the time). I drank quickly and ordered another glass. After my long loneliness, I felt happy and I talked to Carol while Rashid danced with his girlfriend. I talked to Carol nonstop; all the thoughts of Nietzsche, Kierkegaard, and Dostoyevsky that were stored away in my head for the past months came flooding out my mouth.

Carol was looking at me with her green eyes and only spoke to ask a question urging me to speak more. I drank another glass.

We stayed at the café until two in the morning. On the way back we stopped at the diner and drank several cups of coffee. When we returned to the International House, it was approaching four o'clock in the morning. The next day I awoke at noon and I called Carol to meet in the cafeteria. We spent what was left of Sunday together. At night we went to the movies. I did not kiss or touch her at this time, and I think she would have thought that strange or might have felt uncomfortable. But she felt comfortable when I held her in my arms one warm night in the park. . . .

Carol and the spring changed my life. I kept up with my schedule of studies and attended my lectures and conferences. I cut down on my late nights and the nights at the bars drinking. It was not due to my will power (will power is not enough for most situations) but for two reasons: low funds and the thirst for knowledge.

Despite the tight financial situation that persisted from that time until my return to Beirut, the new phase that I entered was peaceful and devoid of the longing for my loved ones and the depression I had experienced in the winter months. When I opened the doors of the International House in the morning, the soft spring breeze met me. As I walked to class with enthusiasm, I greeted all my friends I saw on the way and smiled at everyone. With Carol beside me, I began to sit in the cafeteria where the tables were swarming with students. I participated in conversations and exchanged stories and jokes. It was the same transformation that happens in the life of every Arab student after enduring the long first few months after his arrival in the United States. But my disappointment in America did not change. The American life that the movies and newspapers reported was only a myth. For the movies pictured the American scene not as it is in reality, but as the Americans dream of themselves. The Americans are like us; they don't go to the movies to be reminded that their life is full of hardship and discontent. Instead, they go to escape from it to a beautiful world that Hollywood creates for them.

There is not a single Arab student who does not experience feelings of disappointment after arriving in America. The first disappointment is that they discover that American girls are not all as pretty as they appear in the movies and the magazines. The girls who are very beautiful are difficult to befriend because the competition over them is strong. One must spend months before being able to befriend a reasonably attractive girl. I know young men from Arab countries who have spent years in America without having romantic relationships or sexual encounters.

Beauty, like experience, intelligence, and talent, is a commodity in the United States. It can be bought and sold, not only in the moral sense, but in a materialist way. . . . The most beautiful female students I saw were from Northwestern University, which is close to Chicago. I saw some of them working as dancers in the striptease bars in Kaloomeet, a small town south of Chicago.

I will not forget the first time I went to that town with Fawzi Kahhala, Rashid, and an Iraqi student who was studying ancient history at the University of Chicago (his name was Abd al-Qadir al-Yusuf). Fawzi was older than us and was working in an engineering firm. He owned a new Pontiac in which he took us for rides from time to time, but he forbade us to smoke inside it.

One night Rashid, Abd al-Qadir, and I were sitting in the lobby of the International House, when suddenly Fawzi interrupted us, "Who wants to come see something he's never seen before?"

Rashid said, "And where is this great sight?"

"It doesn't matter where. Are you ready to come or not?"

"We're ready, but tell us where."

"To the striptease bars!"

I did not know what striptease was, so I asked Fawzi. He laughed and said, "You don't know what striptease is? Shame on you, man. Hey guys, get up, let's show Hisham what striptease is."

So we got up to go to the Pontiac, with the fancy leather seats, and made sure to extinguish our cigarettes before getting in. Then we darted south toward the small town, which was approximately 20 miles away.

Fawzi drove us first to a small bar that had a circular bar with a small stage above it. There were no customers, but we sat down and ordered four mugs of beer. It was only a matter of minutes before a slender girl walked onto the stage. Her hair was short and she was very beautiful. She was naked except for a piece of fabric wrapped around her waist. She began dancing to the music played by a band composed of a piano player, a drummer, and a trombonist. We gazed at her from our seats at the bar while she looked down at us from above smiling. When the music reached its height, the girl twirled herself around quickly and took off the small piece of fabric around her waist. Then she left the stage covering her private part with her left hand and waiving the piece of cloth in her right. After a short while, another girl took her place. She was pretty like her, except that she was wearing a long gown. The orchestra started a new tune. The new girl walked around the stage very slowly, then began to take her clothes off piece by piece beginning with her leather gloves. When she got close to her bra, Fawzi could not hold himself back and began to hoot and clap. Rashid, Abd al-Qadir, and I continued looking at her without saying a word. Finally she took off the last piece, except a string around her waist, and continued to dance in front of us. Then she twirled as her friend did and left the stage running while a red light was fixed directly on her behind.

We went to a second and third bar, and saw the same scene in different forms: pretty girls stripped off their clothes to music, then left once the red light was shining directly upon their behinds. Most of all, I remember one of them, she could have been the youngest of them all, with blond hair and fair skin. She came onto the stage in Native Indian garb and began an Indian dance. Every now and then she shouted the cries of a Native Indian. Then she took off her Native garb piece by piece until she reached her bra. Once she unfastened the tie behind her back, her breasts appeared and from each of her nipples hung a red ribbon. Suddenly she began to move her breasts in a circular motion, going up and down to the beat of the music. The ribbons twirled around her nipples like the propellers of an airplane.

The bartender told us that all these strippers were students at Northwestern University who worked in the bars part-time. They received higher pay than in any other job they could get at the university. I asked him about the girl in the Native Indian garb and he told me that she was 18-years-old from Houston, Texas.

For some reason I was not able to forget that girl and her image remains in my mind to this day. I see her in my dreams every now and then, as if I was watching a movie in slow motion. She is just as I had seen her about 30 years ago: completely naked, except for the ribbon in her blond hair, and the two red ribbons circling her breasts.

(When I started writing these pages, my dreams were clouded by past occurrences. Memories returned to me, the ones I thought time had erased . . .). After that I never went to a striptease bar again, except for one last time. That was in New York with Yusuf Khal and Manuel Yunus. What a difference between the atmosphere of the Northwestern student strippers and the professional dancers of 55th Street in New York! But who knows . . . maybe some of the dancers we saw in New York were some of the same ones from Northwestern who failed out of school and could not find any other work beside stripping, which they had only taken up as a hobby in university.

—Translated by Ghada Sobaie

IV

America in the Eyes of
Arab Women Travelers

19.

America and I (1962?)

JADHIBIYYA SIDQI is an Egyptian writer of fiction, and a journalist.
She was a visiting lecturer at the University of Western Illinois, in
Macomb, during the academic year 1960–1961. She published her
absorbing account about her stay in *America and I,* with allusions to
the feature film *The King and I.* The book is dedicated to Egypt and
the front page has a picture of the author in front of the booth that
she set up to represent Egypt in one of the American universities. The
booth shows Egyptian flags with a picture of Nasser and the words
"EGYPT, THE CRADLE OF CIVILIZATION."

I like carrots, celery, lettuce, and everything that is green, but I like them
without anything added to them, without oil, lemon, or salt. I like them
the way they were created by God . . .

When I traveled to America, and its fame for salads is unrivaled, I was
happy that I was going to eat what I liked, and in great quantities. However, it became clear to me that the Americans, even if they were the kings
of salads, make salads that are rich in additives, grease, multicolored oils,
mayonnaise, and heavy sauces of various tastes and a rainbow of colors! Indeed, despite the contents of the bowl, there were always thin slivers of carrots, and celery, and lettuce. But they were lying in the middle of a crowd
of other things, such as shrimps, anchovies, tuna, and pasta. (Yes, I swear to
you, they put pasta in their salad!) Then these greens would be drowned,
soaked for hours in sharp vinegar and a sluggish sauce with its lethal fat
that can simply kill you.

So, I completely refused to eat that American salad.

In the beginning, I was too embarrassed to request something else. And
in the fashion that I like, I maintained patience and self-possession . . . and
with the passage of time, I was afraid that my mind would be enfeebled,
my strength sapped, and that I would have no energy left to keep going.

What was I to do then to maintain my energy and perform my duties? My responsibility here was great. Since it is not in my nature to say no, I found myself agreeing to give a number of lectures on any subject requested of me, in any location, and at any time: night or day, under the heat of the sun or under the pouring rain, or in the middle of one of those famous American storms. I had agreed to lecture anywhere as long as there was a podium and an audience!

Although I am used to working that hard in my life, what would happen if I were robbed of all my strength? What would happen if my mind stopped or slowed down because it was starved of its fuel?

So I anxiously approached the landlady, and asked for plain greenery without their world-famous salad dressings.

When she laughed at me, I felt like a peasant woman who was living in the city for first time and was tired of fancy urban food and started to crave the modest village food.

The landlady laughed at me, but from that moment on she started supplying me with all kinds of wonderful greenery every day: tomatoes, carrots, celery, beets, and cucumbers; there were also some lettuce leaves that climbed on the sides of the plate the way plants climb on the fence of a garden.

The news was spread everywhere. It became known that this was my favorite food and it was served to me night and day. This calmed me and calmed my stomach. However I gained the funny nickname "Rabbit." I didn't get angry though. After all, what's wrong with rabbits?

Sunday, October 8

There are many old maids in America. I met with many of them. It seems that once you arrive at the apex of modernity, decline will have to follow. There is always a trade-off in life, that is the law of nature. Nothing is perfect in this life. In America, you may enjoy the fruits of civilization and modernity and you feel as though you were dreaming with open eyes, and then suddenly, always suddenly, you are shocked to witness the hideous aspects of this unbelievable, magic world, a world brought to you on the wings of imagination.

My God! My heart feels for the harsh loneliness that graces their faces and hearts especially in a place like America, where there is no place for the elderly. I don't mean that they don't find houses to sleep in. On the contrary, there are many places in America, either run by the government or with very low rent, specifically for old men, old women, and old couples. A couple, for example, who have reached old age are able to live in a place for the rest of their days where they will be cared for by nurses and professionals of the highest standard in elderly care. The old couple will find all the amenities of old age such as food, shelter, clothing, and entertainment, and that's all. What do I mean by "and that's all"? Allow me to get to the point. The old man, who has retired from the hardship of work and carries on his shoulders 70 or 80 productive years, can no longer be useful to society. He is considered dead. In this sense there is a fair amount of cruelty in the way the elderly are treated. What makes this cruelty greater is that he is not only considered useless by the government but also by his own family and children.

This is a pervasive problem. Of course, there are those rich, old people who would not think of living in free or subsidized retirement homes. There are old people, whether men, women, widows, or old maids, who live in the lap of luxury. But the hardship, the hardship of loneliness, of being abandoned by their families, is the problem!

The government is able to pass any law, but it is unable to change the character of its society to a certain view of life. The situation in America makes us in the East quite concerned, because we revere parents and parenthood. Of course, in our society there are rare cases where a person kills his parents. But that is deviant. Likewise, in America, there are cases where a son or a daughter reveres his or her parents, but they are a minority. The difference between being a minority and being deviant may be small indeed, but both cases do not represent the majority.

I took advantage of one of those lectures on social issues to insert a few verses of the Quran that deal with parents and parenthood. I told them about the story of Jesus in the Quran and the pains that his mother Mary, peace be upon her, had to endure. I recited these verses several times. I told them that the patience and hard work of the fathers has meant that every generation has been able to survive. I could not overcome a certain sour tone in my voice when I said to them,

> You have asked me to talk about the wisdom of the Pharaonic sage Ptah-Hotip to students of Ancient Egypt. Do you know who this wise man was? Do you know where his knowledge, which transcends the ages, came from? It came from the fact that he was a father, even though he was widely known as a sage and a statesman. All this wisdom was given from father to son, in the hope that the latter would learn from the lessons of history and be able to face the world and its problems. It was a father who etched his wise sayings on Egypt's memory. It was a father who filled his son's ears with intelligence.
>
> From the beginning of time, mothers and fathers possess a sixth sense in regard to their children. So why do you show such lack of respect for your parents?

I went into prolonged discussions where they assailed me with that American logic that convinces so many. But I resisted, because the matter had to do with parents and their place within family life after their hair grays. I refused to accept their arguments, as did my heart, my senses, my logic, and indeed, my humanity.

They told me: "What do we have to do with these elderly people once their role in life has ended? Let them leave us alone with our own problems, our own logic and our own lives!"

Kipling did say the truth: "The East is the East, and the West is the West, and the twain shall never meet."

Monday, October 9

America, as we all know, isn't just a country, it is a continent in itself! It has 50 states, the last that joined the group was Hawaii, and before that was Alaska. The size of the United States is great: it is around 3,300 miles stretching from its eastern to its western shores. The nature of its land changes greatly from one state to the other. Thus, the visitor to America will witness a great diversity among the people themselves. For example, the people of Colorado, in their habits, physical features, and inclinations differ substantially from the people of the valleys and the plains. Americans differ from state to state depending on the predominant environment of their state. The people of Texas, for example, along with their vast grazing plains where they became famous for breeding and trading cattle and horses, are different from the people of another flat state, Illinois, the inhabitants of which are quiet and peace-loving, a people who sanctify married life, who love to visit their neighbor and have small family gatherings.

The area in America that is famous for the cultivation of all types of grain is known as the Corn Belt. When you are in Illinois, you will meet people who are 70 years old and have never left their home state. Even the young people of the state would be filled with anxiety if they had to leave their small towns. If they were offered excellent jobs in another state, they would be leaving their hearts, emotions, and aspirations in the state that witnessed their birth. Their letters to their parents and neighbors would never cease.

Sunday, November 5

Despite the faults of Americans, every day that I spent among them confirms my belief that they are earnest in their desire to rectify these faults and to plug the leaks in their characters and in their culture. They really do try to tackle their innately weak ability to learn different languages. They do not hesitate to harshly criticize government programs from every angle, be it in television talk shows, plays, film, the songs on the radio, magazines, or in newspapers. But there are some traditions and facets of their character that they will never be able to change, or even think of changing. They pride themselves on individual freedom, a complete freedom unencumbered by any responsibility toward parents, society or religion, responsibilities that a person would naturally be slow to assume given the choice. It seems that a lot of American fathers hold on to that freedom out of disillusionment rather than belief. This disillusionment is due to a general lack of understanding with the new generation of youth. This new rebellious generation is the first one to not listen or benefit from their fathers' advice. They have created new rules for society, with perpetually changing standards and ephemeral fashions. Their brand of lunatic music, full of animalistic urges and sexual connotations, has ruffled the feathers of the governments of many nations who have responded to this insidious export with bans and censorship.

These trends that originate from the new generation of youth along with the problems that are not substantial, the misplaced dilemmas, the dance, the music, and the corruptive influences, all these obstruct and pervert America's journey, and place it in an unenviable predicament.

I visited some orphanages full of illegitimate children and shelters for unmarried mothers. I listened to them, spoke to them, and observed them. These shelters are frighteningly widespread. It is true that the rules that are followed in these shelters are of the highest standards. They are humane and exemplary, arousing admiration in their use of the newest and most precise ideas concerning education. There are those who might ask, what is so special about that? In all the countries of the world there occur secret relations between men and women. So why single America out?

It is true that such affairs go on in most countries. But in America these affairs occur frequently, and they are not seen as "strange" or rarities. In America, the doors and opportunities remain open to young girls who have forsaken the rules of their fathers and forefathers and were quick to "experiment" without thinking about consequences. This is the problem! A person who visits these shelters, with their wonderful architecture and facilities, would feel that what the youth of today needs is a heavy hand and some discipline. It is better that such discipline be imposed on the youth of the nation rather than see it collapse under the weight of their mischief.

I am not sure, but I think that modernity after a certain apex must inevitably decline. This, I believe, is the secret of nature. After the peak of youth, old age charts its decline, and after progress, entropy follows. Such is the history of civilizations; they rise and fall.

I feel sad to say that. I hope that I am not right.

—Translated by Shakib Alireza

20.

An Egyptian Girl in America (1983)

KARIMA KAMAL is a young Egyptian who spent several years in the United States where she was a doctoral student at the University of Chicago. Her 1983 book, *An Egyptian Girl in America,* reveals the literary skills of a keen observer of the American scene. The cover of the book shows an enlarged face of an Egyptian woman with a drawing of the Statue of Liberty in the foreground. Her account includes stories about her American classmates, American women, love and marriage the American way, teenage pregnancy in America, and New York City.

America is truly a society without a mask!

It is a society that uncovers its face and in a moment you are able to witness all its shortcomings and virtues. Because it is a face without a mask, it surprises you and shocks you. It even outrages you . . .

America is a society that does not wear a mask because the American fears himself more than he fears God or other people.

The American puts his own interests a thousand times above God or above what others might say. America is a society of individuals who came from around the world and have nothing in common with one another except for a dream that fills their heads and a label for being "an immigrant." They dug in hard and faced a tough life. They made themselves; they did not live at the expense of others. Their experience has been a matter of life or death, surviving or perishing, that is why the American lives his life to the fullest. He tries to enjoy every minute. He refuses to continue in a failing venture, because in his mind he lives once and only once! He enjoys his life and refuses to accept old age. He tries to postpone old age as much as he can, which is why the retirement age in America is 70 years.

Probably from the same desire to enjoy life, the Americans hate to delve into anything outside their work. As a result, American culture is glossed with superficiality to an extent that when I was speaking with a young American man he said in amazement, "Why do you think a lot, and analyze and theorize?" I actually discovered that we Egyptians spend a lot of time thinking and analyzing our own conduct and the conduct of others. This is strange to the American who doesn't usually spend a lot of time thinking and analyzing. Actually he thinks while he walks, or you can say that his steps are an expression of his thinking. So he does not spend a lot of time thinking before making his decision. The American's concept of entertainment is that it must be of great size and great quantity. Even if that enjoyment were an ice cream cone, or a box of popcorn, or a glass of Coca-Cola, it has to be unbelievably gigantic. This American "large-size" concept of entertainment and fun is not found in Europe or any other place for that matter.

This exaggerated need for pleasure is probably what glosses the American culture with superficiality. For example, American television is boring; it rarely grabs you or stimulates your mind. The most interesting and enjoyable part of American television is the news which is covered at times live, at much risk to the news crew, taking you to the scene of the action as though you were living it. It does not matter what the news item is. For example, the war in Lebanon was brought live to America's living rooms. What was happening there was not presented from a piece of paper read by an anchorman. Instead the viewer was able to watch live scenes from the battlefront. The reporter on television was reporting from the middle of Lebanon while the bullets were flying about him and tanks and soldiers were around him.

American politics are similar to the movies. The politicians, local and international, are in the eyes of the American like the Hollywood stars.

The sitcoms and series are all detective stories or "westerns" that do not appeal to you. The strangest thing is that the successful sitcoms that we import from American television are the best that appear on our television sets, albeit these programs are rare in proportion to the long hours and the many channels. There are special cable channels for which you must pay a subscription fee, and they present horror films or sex films. None of it is of good quality at all.

The way Americans enjoy their lives sometimes seems strange. One realizes this during American national holidays. I had firsthand experience celebrating "Taste of Chicago," one way the city of Chicago celebrates the Fourth of July. In the morning, a large group of us from the International House took a train to the center of town where the festival was scheduled to take place. It was in a park that occupies a large space in the city. It is such a large space one cannot imagine that a park could be so big. Within a short amount of time the park was filled with thousands of people. The

American men, women, and children crowded the park, some of them sitting on quilts while others roamed around, but with great difficulty because of the big crowds. There were many stands selling food, drinks, and balloons of different shapes, with faces, stars, and animals drawn on them. Some of the people wore headbands with stars on them, and some drew stars and other colored objects on their faces. The old as well as the young took part in the festivities.

In the amusement park there were carts that sold presents, and there was a big stage on which they sang patriotic songs and the audience sang along with the small band. In the evening fireworks went off. What defines the whole event was one thing: a big crowd, so big that one was crushed in its midst.

People were moving aimlessly in every direction, bumping into each other. They had trouble moving about. They turned into one huge mass that could not do anything except spend money at the food stands. You had to get tickets to buy food and you had to stand in lines to buy certain types of food or a beer. Upon our return near dawn, the street looked as if it had been taken over by mobs. The train station was filled with exhausted people dreaming of their beds, trying to get on the train. They didn't do anything all day except struggle with the crowds and eat different types of food. In conclusion, that was enjoyment à la American style.

Life in America is life on the move, action every moment, work every minute, and decisions every second. You cannot sleep or do anything. What you do for work decides whether you will live or die, whether you will rise to the summit or fall to the abyss of society. In America you do not advance because of seniority or goodwill, and your work controls not only whether you will advance or not but whether you will have an income at all. Otherwise you will be fired and will not be able to go to work the next day. The worst is that you may find yourself on the street without work and without income. This lack of security is what has created all this technology, civilization, and fast progress. The security in our country is what promotes laziness, dependence on others, slow-paced life, and the lack of innovation.

America is freedom . . . progress . . . violence . . . and aggression, all at once!

Freedom in America gives human beings the opportunity to live as they please, and we Egyptians might feel we are deprived of this freedom. In order for us to make a decision, we need to consider a wide range of options and probably ask a lot of people. All the American has to do is search his mind, and he makes his decision without consideration to anyone else. So a lot of ideas disappear in our life and do not get translated into action because of our fear of what others might say.

But freedom in America often kills innocence, the innocence of the young, the innocence of social relations, the innocence of love, and the innocence of feelings. At the same time you envy America for its freedom, you pity her for the price she pays for this freedom.

America is civilization, progress, and technology. Those who say that technology crushes the human, are those who do not know what civilization is or have never experienced it, or do not want to be jealous of American civilization. After my stay in America, I would laugh sarcastically at those who think that civilization destroys humanity. The reality as I witnessed it in America, the country of civilization, is that civilization gives a human an increased sense of individuality, self-confidence, and his own sense of importance.

In this civilization, the American gets compensated unbelievably for trivial losses. It surprises you if you are from the Third World, where there is no surprise or outrage for people who happen to swallow a nail, fall into a gutter, or eat poisonous food. When civilization disappears, the value of a human dwindles. But in America, where civilization reigns, humans become very valuable. Humans are worth more than anything else. For example, if somebody slipped on a stairwell, the designer of the stairs will be sued because they were not designed well. The American gets compensation if his pool was not built the way it was designed, or if he ate in a restaurant and got indigestion. The American will return something he bought from the store, even if he bought it a while ago, because he does not like it. In the store they welcome him as if he has come to buy the whole store, not as if he is there to return a single product. That might be why Americans are very friendly, because there is no pressure and stress on them. The Americans usually carry the smile of contentedness.

You can feel this friendliness in restaurants, in stores, in supermarkets, on the bus, and in the subway. The Americans always use classical expressions to express this friendliness. They always say "good day," "good evening," "have a good time," and all of these have one meaning, which is to wish someone happiness.

Observers of the American scene have different viewpoints about this friendliness. Some say it is a nice way to attract customers, and some say it is the nature of the people, who are united as immigrants and try to overcome their differences. Some say it is only a mask to hide the true American character and nature. Still others say it is friendliness that is not from the heart, insincere. No matter what the truth is about these explanations and analyses, this friendliness makes you feel comfortable and welcomed. You are treated with respect, whether this is out of the desire to deal wisely with others, or out of genuine sentiment.

This friendliness does not extend to people of other nationalities, so the Americans here are not dissimilar to the Nazis.

The German citizen under the Nazis felt that he was the best in the world because of his race. The American feels he is the strongest in the world because he owns the arms, the civilization, the technology, and controls the fate of the world.

The American feels his power and his wealth, but his only weak point is that he has no history. That is why the American is in awe of an old carpet or an antique vase. Even if the antique is of rotted wood or is a faded picture of an old person, they are interested in it. The American tries to convince himself and others that he has history. So in Disney World you find a collection of wooden statues depicting the American presidents. They beam light on these statues and have them speak about their period of governing the United States to give the illusion that the country has an old history.

Everything in America is big: the streets, skyscrapers, glasses of Coca-Cola, bags of popcorn, and glasses of beer. The one thing here that comes in small amounts is respect. The American does not have to respect anyone. He does what he wants, says what he wants, and moves around in the way he wants. I wonder whether it is an excessive respect for his individual freedom or a rejection of all the traditions of the Old World in the New World.

America is aggressive. America is a society that is used to aggression. So they listen to news about crimes in the same way they listen to the weather forecast. Most of these incidents appear strange to any foreigner. For example, one day American television reported two bizarre incidents. The first one was in Miami. One of the workers in a factory did not like the work shifts, so he shot and killed nine people and wounded three others. In the second incident, a man kidnapped two young girls and raped them.

We should ask ourselves, is crime in American society more frequent and more dangerous than it is in any other society? Or does it just appear that way because everything is reported and not concealed?

If the crime situation in the American society appears strange, the condition of the law is stranger. The accused will not be convicted unless there is absolutely no doubt he committed the crime. If he was caught committing the crime, he gets out of it by claiming psychological insanity, as John Hinckley did when he shot President Reagan.

In no other country can you shoot at a president and not get sentenced to life imprisonment. Only in America, where the television cameras filmed Hinckley shooting President Reagan, could he be found not guilty and sent for psychological treatment. Who knows what he is capable of doing after he is let out. . . .

❧　❧　❧

No matter how long your trip to America is, when it is time to leave and you gather all your belongings, your feeling of homesickness that was with you throughout your trip will be replaced with a new feeling of sadness. It is sadness for leaving a place that is dear to you, a place that has become part of your life. You are leaving an experience that filled your life for some time. You are leaving a lot of memories, moments of discovery, sadness, happiness, homesickness, and a sense of acceptance as well as repulsion. You are still searching for an answer to the question that was on your mind when you first set foot in America. A world completely different from yours and the question is, which world do you prefer?

Your world suffers from the lack of freedom, and this world suffers from excessive freedom. Your world suffers from being under-civilized, and this world suffers from over-civilization. Your world suffers from a lack of seriousness, and this world suffers from too much seriousness. Is it the fate of the human beings to go on comparing and complaining? It seems to me that we will continue to complain because there is no country that will give us the right solution; the only solution is the one we will find within ourselves.

—Translated by Dima Reda

21

The Trip:
The Days of an Egyptian Female Student in America (1987)

RADWA ASHUR is an Egyptian academic who specializes in American literature. Between 1973 and 1975 she was a doctoral student in Afro-American studies at the University of Massachusetts, Amherst. Currently she teaches at Ayn Shams University in Cairo. Her elegant 1987 book, *The Trip: The Days of an Egyptian Student in America,* which ran into its third edition, provides the reader with a sober account of the life of a foreign student in an American academic institution.

The seven o'clock news televised a report about streaking and how it was becoming a widespread social phenomenon among university students. The students of North Carolina University broke the record when one day more than three hundred male and female students came running outside together, completely naked. Once the news media reported about that event, many people became very interested knowing more about it. Not a day passed without advertisements covering the university declaring that the students of Southwest University had decided to stage a "streaking" festivity. The festivity was a communal denudation in which a horde of nude participants would run outside at 11 at night from a given point on campus to the center of campus, and back again. This news excited all of us at the university, those who wished to take part in it and those who wished only to observe. As for us, the group of foreign friends, we laughed like a bunch of old fogies and said, "Why don't we have a small private party for the occasion? We'll drink, eat, and dance in the study hall that overlooks campus. At the moment of the event, we can observe it all from the windows and thereby we won't miss this intriguing event!"

When I saw my Iranian friends arrive armed with a camera, I said, "I see that you will be taking indecent pictures!"

I laughed, and one of them responded laughing, "No, just pictures that record the time and place!"

"Honestly, I tell you what amazes me more than the thought of these youths stripping for no understandable reason is that they will be exposed to the bitter cold. They will all wake up with pneumonia tomorrow!"

We didn't talk about the event after that. Instead we discussed other topics, trying to forget the crucial event of the evening, until we actually did forget it.

"Here, they are beginning to come out now!" I do not know who had made the window into a spy tower, but we all ran to the windows to look at the large horde of stark naked students hurrying out of the back doors of Prince House wearing only socks and shoes. I wondered whether their great speed was because of the extreme cold or because of their embarrassment at their unusual nudity. Never in my entire life have I seen a scene like this or anything close to it, so I said, "We should have gone down to see them up close."

A German friend said, "But the weather is too cold."

My friend responded to me laughing, "Nothing is stopping you from running down after them now!"

We were still hanging around the windows commenting on the scene when Mary and Sheila, who lived on the same floor, entered screaming madly. Mary said with her deep, booming voice, "What a sight! We wore our jackets and went downstairs and saw them pass by in front of us."

I laughed with a mixture of nervousness and amusement at the situation. Mary continued, "I took pictures of them! All their bodies were shivering from the extreme cold. Poor students! As for the guys . . . Oh my God!"

She left laughing. Sheila talked to another group about her amazement at the number of the nudes. It was obvious that there were hundreds. Sheila said confidently, "It wasn't less than four hundred students!"

The next day I sat in the English department with the professor of critical theory and another friend, waiting for the rest of the group to go to the professor's house for a lecture. The university's newspaper had published a report about the event, and said that the number of students was close to four hundred. A picture of some naked girls running in the crowd was published on the front page. The professor said smiling quietly "a new trend," and I said to myself, "What is it that generates these new trends of madness?"

The answer was clear in the next day's paper of the *Daily Collegian*. One of the representatives of the Amherst police, which the university places under its jurisdiction, said, "Why should we worry? The students are having a fun time. This is healthy, and it is surely better than the political frenzy that overtook them in the sixties."

The police wanted the students to enjoy their time like this because it was beneficial, but if an individual went beyond this it would be another matter. For that reason, two days later, the police apprehended a student who decided to run naked on campus at noon. The police caught him, threatened him with punishment and then let him go.

—Translated by Ghada Sobaie

22.

America's Other Face (1991)

LAYLA ABU ZAYD is a Moroccan writer, journalist, and broadcaster. In 1983, she published in Arabic *The Year of the Elephant,* which was published in an English translation by the University of Texas Press in 1989. Her book, *America's Other Face,* was issued in two editions, one in 1989 and the other in 1991. The cover of the book shows the negative of the Statue of Liberty holding a missile instead of the torch. The topics of this account include: American mass media, Arabs and Islam in America, American feminism, the poor in America, and education in America.

As an Arab, I stood by the Iraqi people [during the Gulf War in 1991]. The reasons for my stand were simple: Do I support the one who strikes at Israel and America and punishes both for the first time in 42 years for the crimes they committed against the Palestinians? Or, do I support those who fight on the side of America and Israel and allow our sacred lands (in Arabia) to become the military camps of polytheists, to be trampled under their army boots, and to be littered with their beer cans? . . .

I still remember the crisis I faced when I went to perform the [Islamic] pilgrimage in 1977 [in Saudi Arabia] because I did not have a [male] guardian even though I was accompanied by my mother. Then I was told, "this measure is necessary in this country." If that was the case then why was it that the American female soldiers who came to Saudi Arabia [during the Gulf War] were not accompanied with male guardians? Was it necessary for the Saudis to bring in American women in order to defend Saudi men, the same men who regard women as a thing that must be totally covered in wraps, long sleeves, and veils? Did America really need to bring women to Arabia to defend the Saudis or did they do it on purpose with the intention of humiliating the Saudis? It looks like the Saudis act so arrogantly only toward us [Arab women]. May Allah guard me against their arrogance! A Saudi once said to me: "Next time you come to Saudi Arabia bring with you an American male so if the Saudis ask you 'Where is your male guardian?' you can say, 'Here he is!'" I said to the Saudi, "I have no desire to go back [to Saudi Arabia]; thanks to the Americans, these lands are no longer sacred."

—Translated by Kamal Abdel-Malek

23.

America the Way It Is (1995)

HALA SARHAN is an Egyptian who came to the United States on a scholarship to study drama at the University of Louisville, Kentucky, where she graduated with a doctorate in the early 1990s. The account she published in her 1995 book, *America the Way It Is,* is narrated with warmth, humor, and a tinge of satire. The cover shows the drawing of a woman in torn jeans and sneakers and with a hot dog sandwich in her hand, with the skyline of a city that looks like New York. Some of the topics covered are: American classmates, American professors, American weather, American cuisine, "All You Can Eat" restaurants, the American Dream, buying on credit in America, and snow in America.

The American Dream

America is practically a continent, not a mere country. The East Coast is more than 4,000 kilometers from the West coast and it takes eight hours for an airplane to cover the distance between Washington, D.C., and San Francisco. The citizens of the East Coast live with snow-covered mountains and temperatures well below zero while on the same day the citizens of the West Coast in Los Angeles sit on the beach enjoying the warmth of the sun. Meanwhile, in the desert of Arizona and Nevada, the temperature bakes the skin and in the cold forests of Montana the people are clothed in thick fur coats. The geographical extent of the American continent to the east, west, north, and south, along with the difference in the composition of the environment, from mountains, to valleys, to deserts, to forest, and to beaches, is reflected in large behavioral inconsistencies in the American personality. Therefore, it is difficult to summarize the characteristics in the American personality. The East Coast is the land of conservatives, intellects, and artists. The personality of a New Yorker in the Northeast where life is fast, noisy, crowded, and hectic and marked by

crime, flourishing art, and extreme freedom differs from the personality of
a citizen living in Palm Springs, where life is comfortable and tranquil.
Furthermore, these two are different from the citizen of the West Coast
from Los Angeles or San Francisco, where there is spontaneity, liberty, un-
inhibitedness, Hollywood, ambition, and eccentricity. Geography definitely
conditions personality in each one of them. In addition there are large cultural, artistic, and religious differences among the American citizens.

The citizen who is of European origins is different from the citizen
who is of Chinese origins, or Latino (from Latin America), or Mexican
origins. There was an American citizen who lived 70 years of his life without ever traveling from Texas to Seattle because the distance was five hours
by plane or a number of days by car. I still remember the look of respect
and admiration given to me by a drama professor from the University of
Louisville in the state of Kentucky because I made a visit to New York and
saw a Broadway play. I was the newcomer from a Pharaonic country and
he was the American who spent 50 years of his life in the United States,
but in all his days he had not set foot in New York City.

From then on I found many Americans who did not know a thing
about the world outside America. They imagined that world was America
and that America was the world. If you asked one of them "What is the
capital of Syria? Or Finland?" he would not even know that there was a
country with that name. The popular American saying that expresses this
logic is rather telling: "Far from my Bed." This is when he wants to say that
a thing does not concern him in the least. There is no doubt that those
who said that geography is the guide history and politics follow are completely correct. On the right of America is the Atlantic Ocean, which was
crossed by boats in ten days and on her left is the Pacific Ocean, which was
crossed by boats in two weeks. Naturally the concept of the country, the
nation, and the continent all carry a different meaning in America than in
any other place. The homeland in the American imagination is not a
homeland as the Egyptian or the Indian understands it. There are American citizens who have lived and died having seen only five American states
and do not know anything about the other forty-five. Naturally this diverse geography creates rifts in dispositions and makes for contradictory
social behavior. There is the cold personality in the mountains of Vermont
in the northeast. There is the burning personality of southern Arizona in
the southwest, and of course there is the crazy Californian.

In the agricultural areas such as the states of Kentucky and Indiana, there
still are solid families with family values. In the big crowded cities such as
New York, Los Angeles, and Houston, we find a greater amount of disinte-
grated families. In the cities, individualistic and selfish behavior emerges and
the psychologists live a luxurious and carefree life because of them.

The American people continue dreaming the "American Dream." It is a historical expression passed down from generations and favored by every American citizen. The immigrants arrive in America carrying the dream, but what is the American Dream? It is luxury, wealth, freedom, democracy, success, ambition, social mobility, and every story of success. The American Dream is arriving empty-handed from poor, oppressive, primitive countries and toiling, exhausting oneself, working, and becoming a millionaire from the sweat of one's brow and not through inheritance or sudden wealth. The American Dream is to become a senator, congressman, or the president of the United States through free election and not through connections and corruption.

The American Dream is a philosophical, political, economic, and social theory.

—Translated by Nora Kruk

V

Satirical Views of America

24

Cheerful America of the Past:
Journal of a Penniless Student
in the United States (1989)

MUSTAFA AMIN was one of Egypt's best known newspaper editors. In the 1940s, he co-founded *Akhbar al-Yawm*, an Egyptian daily, and for many years was its editor. His 1989 book, *Cheerful America of the Past: Journal of a Penniless Student in the United States,* records his student life in the United States in the 1930s. Apart from its historical value his book is a fine example of humorous writing in Arabic. The cover has an American flag with a smiling round face looking like the disc of the sun with hair looking like sun rays. Some of the chapters in the book are: Wonders in the Land of Wonders, the American Woman, the American Family, American Millionaires, Nighttime in America, Hollywood, and American Festivals.

Our Girls and Uncle Sam's Girls

Now what is the condition of the American woman? When our friend [the author referring to himself in the third person] traveled to America, he was sent off with wishes of safety and strict orders to avoid Uncle Sam's girls, as a healthy person would be advised to avoid the plague. He was advised to close his eyes when a woman winked at him. All he could do if he saw eyes full of the angelic charms, or two lips attracting him like a magnet and eyes dazzling him like the lighthouse of the Egyptian city of Port Said, or bodies strutting around like a peacock or bending like a jasmine branch rustled by the fresh breezes would be to take refuge in God and read the special Quranic verses against magic seven times.

He used to believe that Uncle Sam's women could steal the souls of men like a thief in the night and seize their hearts with the speed of a freight train. His friends saw him off, feeling sorry for him, after they advised him to defend himself, against the eyes and the lips, until his last breath.

But Uncle Sam's girls completely dashed the hopes and ideals that his respected friends built up for him. The American woman does not love to live, rather she lives to love. She believes that love is the one pleasure in life, like smoking or drinking whiskey. Just as every person picks his type of cigarette, the woman picks the type of man she likes.

The girls in Egypt don't require a large financial investment. The young man does not need to do more than wait for an hour when she is tardy or send a moving letter expressing that he is worn out by unrequited love. He only needs to invest in a gallon of gas; or a horse-drawn carriage, if the beloved is from a wealthy family; or a tram ticket for six Egyptian pennies, if Juliet is from a poor family.

It's unfortunate for the Romeo who wants to meet Juliet in America, because he must meet her in front of her family and her relatives, not in the absence of eyes and guardians. He makes an entrance through a door and does not jump over the fence as our friend did with the neighbor girl.

Given this, any honored Romeo will not be successful if he enters Juliet's house with empty hands and only with polite greetings. Instead he must carry a bouquet of flowers. Consequently, I learned that the price of one flower in New York is half a riyal [approximately $0.50] and the cheapest bouquet of flowers is a pound [approximately $2.50]. So now you ought to know, dear reader, that bankruptcy has room for everyone.

The father, or mother, or even the brother opens the door, but they do not greet you with canes and broomsticks. The families of American girls are civil and they greet you with hundreds of "We missed you!" and "We enjoyed your company."

Then you take the lovely woman to the cinema. On the "walk" to the cinema, between the entrance price and taxis, you have to cough up three riyals, or sixty piasters in the currency of the Ottoman times.

After that, Romeo invites Juliet to dinner, because the protocol of Uncle Sam's girls stipulates that if a young man wants to meet a woman, he must invite her to dinner. There are no negotiations except after dinner.

Dinner in America is expensive and there are no modest restaurants in New York. If you want to act humbly and go to a "modest restaurant," you pay no less than five riyals of the bill for yourself and five more riyals on behalf of your beautiful date.

As for the cost of a simple bill, the rendezvous that you would pay five Egyptian pennies for, sets you back five pounds in America.

American women are charming, seductive, and surprising. They fill their elegant social gatherings with laughter and joy.

But Egyptian young women exceed them in charm and allure. There is nectar-like sweetness in their smiles, and melody and music in their laughs. A man can feel this when he sits next to an Egyptian young woman. The electricity and attraction runs through every part of their body. Our friend acknowledges that our Egyptian young women are certainly liars, most certainly selfish, and absolutely certainly deceptive. Yet with all these defects the Egyptian woman excels over any woman in the world in allure, beauty, and sheer seductiveness.

The American woman exceeds the Egyptian woman in her choice of men. She does not like slimy men as do most girls today, who are more concerned with filling the empty holes in their hearts as if they were filling empty jars!

Most Egyptian women consider an effeminate man the best example of a man. One that has lustrous hair, fair skin, reddish cheeks, and a comb he pulls out of his pocket every five minutes to comb his precious hair in front of the mirror. And when he walks, he sways and struts.

But the American woman wants a real man, with a rough voice and masculine character. In America, "Don Juan" is the strong man who hits his girlfriend when she quarrels. He is the one who leads her around and forces his will upon her.

Our friend remembers a famous cinema actress who said to him in the midst of her talk on men whom she admires: "I often feel that the slaps my boyfriend places on my face are more delicious than some of his kisses!"

All young women in America, rich or poor, work. Even Roosevelt's daughter worked in a store selling dresses. Every young woman claims "complete independence" in her house and this is total freedom, freedom to come and go, freedom to receive uncensored, unopened letters but, if she abuses this freedom, the father usually enforces a curfew. Sometimes the matter ends with her expulsion from her family. The young American woman does not burden her family with the cost of her clothes, rather she works to buy pretty clothes for herself.

Our friend thinks Egyptian women have an elegant choice of attire. He does not exaggerate if he says that Egyptian women dress with an elegance that surpasses many movie stars, except that many of them spend a pathetically long time in the bathroom. If the young Egyptian woman cut back in her lying, her deceitfulness, and her makeup, she could not be more radiant.

Finishing Schools

Marriage has become a science in America and one can study it in some universities as one would science, engineering, agriculture, or chemistry. There are special colleges for studying this fine art. In most classes female students sit with male students, but in the required classes they segregate the sexes.

Our friend went to one of these special classes for women. The subject of the lesson was "surprises." The female professor explained to the female students: "Marriage fails when it falls into routine. The husband, who spends ten years in a life that does not change, and does not begin to change, cannot bear it. The husband is almost at the point of knowing what he will eat every day, and what his wife will say. This is why it is good if the wife tries to change!"

The teacher advised her class full of wives to change their married lives and said to them, "Your husband will be bored when he sees that the furniture of the house does not change, the armchair in the right corner, the couch in the left corner, the table in the middle, the radio between the couch and the armchair! The wife must move the furniture around from time to time so the husband feels he is in a new house! The husband will complain about the change at first, but will not continue to feel that he is being moved from atmosphere to atmosphere!"

The teacher advised the wife to surprise her husband by secretly economizing on private expenses from the expenditures of the house. Then she should say to her husband that night, "Let's go to the movies tonight. It's my treat!" or "I would like to invite you to dinner with me!" Or get a present on a special occasion. These trivial surprises make the husband feel that his life does not follow a routine. The husband who is accustomed to always paying the bill is happy when he is invited to dinner once a month on his wife's bill!

Our friend went to a class on "trivial things," and that was not the subject of the class! The teacher said that the most trivial things usually spoil married life. For example, a wife forgets to fix the button of the pants that the husband asked to be fixed and it is turned into a talk about divorce! The husband realizes as he is at work, or riding the train, that his wife forgot this simple, trivial request that he made. All day he says to himself, "Oh what a careless wife! She forgot my pant's button. Why did I marry her?" Then the husband returns to his house irritated, and the debate starts between the married couple. Many end in argument or divorce, but it is up to the wife to be concerned with the trivial things that her husband requests of her. She must be careful not to forget, and it is up to her to record the orders of her husband on a piece of paper. How happy would a husband feel when his wife bows in front of him in the morning and says to him, "What are your orders today, Your Majesty?" The man feels some pride and joy and feels he is really a king.

Our friend went to a third class called "bad habits," and the teacher reminded the students that most wives are accustomed to asking their husband what he would like prepared for dinner the moment after he finishes his breakfast! This is a foolish question, for the husband cannot think about dinner while he is stuffed from breakfast! The teacher recommends that rather than forcing foods that her husband does not like on him she should know what he likes and prepare it for him.

On this matter, our friend thought it was fortunate that in most cases in America wives cook food by themselves. Therefore the kitchens, which are operated by electricity, are the cleanest rooms in the house. They are so clean that in most wealthy houses the family members have breakfast in the kitchen! Is there any one of us in an Eastern country that can enter his kitchen to have breakfast in it?

The American wife boasts that she makes the food that she feeds her husband with her own hands, and there is no cook in the house. If a newspaper talks about a rich man, it says there is a private cook in his house!

The American wife goes out by herself to buy the meat and vegetables. In America there are stores where you can buy meat, vegetables, fruit, milk, butter, and bread, all in one place. It is easy for the wife to order from the store on the phone and say I want this and this. Then within five minutes the store assistant knocks on the kitchen door carrying what she wants. In most cases, wives in America are workers. American companies produce canned goods that can be cooked quickly, and in ten minutes the wife can prepare your food. It is not as it is in the East, where the wife stays in the kitchen from the morning until two in the next morning preparing the food. At this point you cannot see her until you find the smell of *mulukhiyya* [Egyptian traditional dish] reeking from her!

One of the most shameful habits our friend remembers hearing the American teacher explain to her students was the wife pointing out to her husband the quarrels that happened during the day between the children, neighbors, or hired help. The teacher said, "The smile is a secret weapon that the wife can conquer her husband with." The husband returns from his work exhausted and you should not increase his troubles by telling him yours.

The teacher advised wives not to take off their clothes in front of their husbands. There must always be some formality between them. It must always be the wife's right to hide from her husband when she wants to beautify herself, because one does not find the lamb slaughtered and cooked in one's presence delicious. Therefore, the wife must not reveal the secret of her beauty to her husband and must surprise him!

Our friend left this finishing school disappointed that there is no equivalent in the East where teachers teach women the art of marriage. Everything an Eastern woman learns, she hears from her mother or her older sister. Therefore, she becomes miserable if her mother was miserable. She enters a new life without learning the psychology of marriage.

In America there are statistics on wives and housework. In the February 1944 *Look* magazine it was reported that every American wife washes 26,280 plates by hand a year! In America a hundred thousand wives use dishwashers, while the rest of the wives wash the dishes by hand. Hired help does not take care of this work except in rich houses. The wife washes between 20 to 30 pounds of clothes every week by hand.

Of the 30 million houses in America, there are 28,738,203 houses with radios. Curiously, the soap companies broadcast small operas on the radio during the time that an American wife is usually doing her household wash. She turns on the radio to listen to cheerful widow songs as she cleans her children's pants and her husband's shirts. There is no maid in America that comes to the houses to wash the family clothes, as is the case among us in the East, rather the American wife assumes this honor herself.

Evidence of the wealth of the American family is that before the war there were 22 million cars. That is to say, nearly every family owned a private car.

The newspaper also mentioned that the average American wife mends 347 socks yearly, and most of her dresses and her children's clothes are made by her.

One of the good things about an American wife is that she acts "young" with her children. She plays with them, runs with them, rides bikes, greets them, and does not feel the difference in age between her and her children.

Some curious statistics: the American wife kisses her husband around 1,500 times a year regardless of her age, stands in front of the mirror 182 hours a year, spends 35 hours a year at the hairdresser, polishes her nails 45 times a year, and brushes her teeth 500 times a year!

—Translated by Nora Kruk

25

America, You Cheeky Devil (1990)

MAHMUD AL-SADANI is a popular Egyptian satirical writer and journalist. With his characteristic biting sarcasm, he offers in his 1990
book, *America, You Cheeky Devil,* a portrait of America that is at times
critical but not devoid of humor. The cover shows a drawing of the
Statue of Liberty but with a man's face wearing a crown studded with
fountain pens and holding instead of the torch a match in one hand
and a matchbox in the other. Some of the topics in the book are: the
dollar cult in America; gangs; Arabs in America; the American Dream.

The American Era

America is the greatest, largest, and most obnoxious empire in history.
As for being the greatest, imagine this: it managed to reduce its de-
fense budget this year by $160 billion after having reached an agreement
with the Soviet Union. America is large; she is a country without bound-
aries. She is the size of 50 countries and her people are a mix of all the
peoples of the earth. As an example of her obnoxiousness, despite her
greatness she continually claims that the Israeli lobby manipulates her resources and decision-making. She is extremely angered if one of the Emirates buys a shipment of knives from China, but will turn right around and
congratulate Israel on firing missiles into outer space. The proof of America's obnoxiousness is that all her leaders, without exception, when they are
still in office they side with the Israelis, and then side with the Arabs once
they are out of office. She invades Panama, a country the size of New York
state, under the pretense that Panama's president, Noriega, trades in drugs,
even though the real reason behind her invasion of Panama is to control
and occupy the Panama Canal forever. America attacked Cuba one day on
the pretense that Castro was a dictator, even though she has diplomatic relations with the dictator of El Salvador and supports the dictator of South

Africa. America has been shedding tears over human rights abuses in Ro-
mania and Poland for years now, even though her heart has not skipped a
single beat for the loss of human rights in Israel! She is the leader of the
democratic world, even though she is angered by the victory of democracy in Chile, plotted against it, and overthrew the elected representative,
Allende, by attacking his palace with bombs and killing him in the aftermath! She is the leader of the free world, even though her agents in most
parts of the world reign with steel and fire. She represents the mission
against drugs in the world, while she sells drugs of exceptional quality on
the world market in order to buy weapons for the Contra army waging a
revolution in Nicaragua.

Basically America is the most obnoxious empire the history of the
human race has ever known. The American market is the largest trade market in the world and her internal democracy is the most widespread
democracy that any of the peoples of the world has ever known.

Any American citizen or American resident is capable of publishing a
newspaper, creating a political party, inventing a new religion, directing a
broadcast station, or owning a station that can broadcast any kind of television program. The American press is capable of overthrowing the president
of the United States. As the richest country in the world, America has produced the greatest sports heroes; created the greatest cinematic and theater
art, which has no comparison in the world; and provided great opportunities for philosophers and scientists. America is a leader in the field of hotel
management and frozen foods, and is the number one country in the world
for its use of domestic flights (though its international flights are unreliable).
In America there are gangs so clever they can steal the kohl eyeliner from
the eye and Mafia gangsters so well-connected they can direct political
campaigns to help you go all the way to the Congress or even the presidency. In America there is corruption you have never seen the likes of before in the past or will ever see in the future. You can buy off members of
Congress, a member in a company's board of directors, the governor of the
state, the local chief of police, the writers, and the gun-toting criminals, but
oh may the sweet mercy of God help the one caught in bribery or the one
who is unlucky enough to end up in an American jail.

Basically America is not a country but a continent. America is not a part
of the human race but it envelopes all of humanity, with its greatness and
depravity, its justice and injustice, its excess and moderation, its wealth and
poverty, and its generosity and avarice. As opposed to previous empires, if
she falls, the entire world will fall with her, because her economy affects
the entire world. Her dollar is the official currency of the globe. A dollar
deposited in a bank anywhere in the world will be recorded in the ledgers
of the American Federal Reserve.

She is the only "tough guy" in the New World, like the late Ibrahim Karum, the greatest of Cairo's tough guys. She has succeeded in eliminating all other bullies by pushing them out of her way and stepping on them with her feet. May the sweet mercy of God help any leader who stands in the path of America's greed, challenges her will, or strays from her path. Sometimes she involves herself with her own boys, and sometimes she uses her allies, such as Israel against the Arabs, the government of Pretoria against Africa, Pakistan against Afghanistan, El Salvador against Nicaragua, Guatemala against Cuba, Taiwan against China, and South Korea against North Korea!

America is the only country that calls her government an administration, because she is not a nation but a company. Her citizens are not a people but shareholders, and every shareholder can expand his share by buying more. Some participants' luck runs out and they lose everything including their name and are transformed into wanderers and beggars. Woe to those who fall into the gutters because companies have no heart and personal interests are the rules of the game. One has to defend one's interests with a firm hand, or with the barrel of a gun. Therefore there is no room for a fair solution to any problem and the only hope is to turn to the American justice system for problems. American justice leans toward the powerful and against the weak. It is a justice that resembles the law of the jungle. With such law there is no possibility that the wild donkey will beat the lion, or the rabbit will beat the wolf, or that the gazelle will speak with the tiger, and for the one who wants to protect his rights, he must have fangs and claws and roar like a lion. But the majority on this earth has no hope and no way out, except that they accept America's decree and abide by its principles, or they ask America to protect them in return for their obedience.

The bad luck of our generation is that we have lived during the American era and have fallen under American justice. We have tasted some of the American benefits in the Sheratons and Kentucky Fried Chickens. The worst part is that we have lived to see the "perestroika" of Gorbachev. The Soviet empire was nothing more than a scarecrow. It was a shaky ruse used by poor nations against American oppression. It was a rusty weapon, but despite its rustiness it was capable of protecting the frightened. Then came perestroika, which pulled down the scarecrow, destroyed the last fence, and broke the bad weapon. The yard is now empty except for America's bullies and their goons.

But, as the Arabic saying goes, something good may still come out of a bad situation. According to God's law, everything will perish except God. As the poet said, "There is always something missing for everything." A saying goes, "The bird flew and reached highest point and will now have to descend." The law will be applied to the American empire as it has been applied to all other empires, and the same will happen in life as it occurs on stage. When things reach an extreme, the breakdown begins. I think we are witnessing the beginning of the end. All we desire is that the saying "Don't be happy to see the bad guy leave before you see who will replace him" does not happen. We implore the Lord that the coming era will be better than the American era, and that humanity will enjoy a new era. An era where each will get his right and everyone is equal in rights and duties. We hope that the coming era will be the human era and not the imperial era. We will never attain this unless we manage a "United States of the globe," where we abolish borders, passports, local currency, and believe that the goods of the earth are for all its inhabitants.

Is this believer in God dreaming?

I think this is what will happen in the next hundred years. When the time comes, the religion will be God's, and the earth will be everyone's.

Oh merciful, oh compassionate Lord, deliver us from the American era.

Now that we have explored the country of Uncle Sam, its east and west, and have lived with its rich and poor, spoken with its educated and ignorant, seen its advantages and disadvantages, and found out that it has opposed us because we are against ourselves, I have prayed to God Almighty that we profit from the good that they have and that we avoid their evil. America, like any other place, is neither all good nor all evil, but because it has everything, its good outdoes its evil.

Now as I prepare to leave, I have nothing left to say but . . . how picture-perfect America is. May God bestow blessing upon blessing upon her.

Everything is abundant, everything is available, and everything is at the reach of those who want it. Rivers . . . what is the Congo compared to hundreds of rivers? Channels . . . the canal of *Sabk* cannot compare to hundreds of American canals. Lakes . . . the Crocodile Lake cannot compare to the thousands of American lakes. There are also fields of trees, fruits of every kind, animals of all shapes, and birds of every color. The animals from the hyena, to the tiger, to the wild turkey, so many that turkey and not mutton is used for big feasts of the month. Strangely enough, there is a holiday celebrated in America in honor of the turkey. The story goes that the pioneers, when they reached the shores of America, faced the terrible fate of near starvation. The water surrounded them on all sides, storms hit them from all directions, and the skies bombarded them with stones of ice. There was nothing to eat and no hope of finding any food. The vegetation was frozen over and the animals fled because of the extreme cold and hunger. Even the birds disappeared and immigrated to a safe haven. In the midst of all this great terror and haunting death, ten young pioneers volunteered to go in search of food. They left exhausted by the snow and drenched with mud. Two days passed and despair almost killed them. Hunger blinded them so they lost their sense of balance and their way home. They were unable to return to tell the others that the land they had come to was not the land of milk and honey, but rather the land of ice and mud; the new land was not the Promised Land, but rather the land of death. On the road back, they were out of breath, and their patience had run out. All hope was extinguished. Then, suddenly, a flock of wild turkeys appeared. It was apparent that the turkeys were also hungry and had gone out in search of food. The two hungry groups faced one another and fought to determine which would eat the other: the battle of man versus the turkey. It was a bloody battle where bones were broken and heads bashed, and it ended with grenades and bullets. A number of the turkeys fled. Finally, by following the moon, the men returned to the refugee camp with hundreds of turkeys. There they ate and drank their fill, and after that they lived off another species called the Indians! Americans celebrate the wild turkey every year. They celebrate it, but the situation has changed and so has the turkey. Americans are no longer suffering from hunger and the turkey is no longer wild. The turkey's nails have been broken and its beak has lost its sharpness, and it has become like the village hens, extremely kind and obedient. The wild turkey has disappeared from America and has left no trace except in remote areas. The number of wild turkeys does not exceed a hundred! The place of the turkey in the wild animal kingdom has disappeared, even though it is still populated with all kinds of other wild animals . . . such as the coyote, the hyena, wild birds, and human beings!

If America is the land of abundance, then it is also the land of vast expanses. From New York to Colorado it is four hours by jumbo jet, which is the same as the distance from Tripoli to Kuwait. From Colorado to Texas it is an hour and a half, which is the same as the distance from Bahrain to Baghdad. From Texas to Los Angeles it is two and a half hours, which is the same as the distance from Cairo to Riyadh. From Washington to San Francisco it is seven and a half hours, which is the same as the distance from Abu Dhabi to Casablanca. Despite the distance there is no one to stop you or search you, no customs or passports. The land of God for the people of God. Every citizen here is free, traveling as he pleases and as he is capable. Tickets are expensive and spending is frequent, but the American has money. His salary provides enough for him for living and traveling expenses. The reason is that the unity of this nation, which spreads from the Atlantic Ocean to the Pacific Ocean, is one piece without divisions and separations. In summer, New Mexican watermelons cover all of the United States; Californian grapes are available in summer and autumn; and Colorado oranges cover the United States in summer and winter. None of

the states give and take fines or complications, even though the difference
between the states is larger than the difference between our countries.
There are more differences in their accents than in our countries. The
Texan cannot be understood by the New Yorker, and the Virginian cannot
understand the Arizonan. The pace of life in Denver differs from the pace
of life in Buffalo, but there is an understanding. Interests are the same and
everyone is rewarded. In America there are a multiplicity of nations, people from Aryan origins and Indian, blacks from Africa, and a large population of "yellows," from China, Japan, and Southeast Asia. In America
Arab-Americans, American Jews, and Spaniards still speak their native languages. America has a multiplicity of religions. There are Buddhist temples
everywhere, synagogues built in all places, mosques rising up to the sky,
and churches of every kind and of every color. There are hundreds of religions and thousands of religious sects; there are people who worship the
tree or the cow, people who pray facing the pyramids. Yet despite all this,
they are all one nation. We are twenty states, a hundred emirates, one million directions, and one hundred and fifty million eternal rulers. To top it
all, we dream of returning to the past and of entering paradise!

The American states became united, and as a result each and every
American became free and responsible. The government is merely a su-
pervisor managing the national affairs, and is not to be the master of its
subjects. The American president is a mere employee who can be kicked
out of office, and whose services can be dispensed of at any moment. He
is not like the omnipotent ruler of the people with divine right, who
curses those who oppose him, banishes those who stand up to him, and
deems those who raise an arm in protest a conspirator, a traitor and a spy,
and without the authentic village morals [a sly reference to one of the oft-
quoted phrase of the late Egyptian president, Anwar Sadat]. Everything is
as it should be. It is not 100 percent but 70 percent and this is good
enough. The government governs with 51 percent of the votes, not 99 percent, or 999 per 1000 as it is in our countries. Every accused is innocent
until proven guilty, and every American is free until the judge gives his ver-
dict. Every American is respected even when he is imprisoned. I wish to
live and see this day in our countries, but it seems like I will need the life-
time of Noah to see the dawn of that day.

I dreamt of that day as I was strolling by the Pacific Ocean between Los
Angeles and San Francisco. I dreamt of it as I was preparing to depart from
America after having been there for six weeks, which I spent mostly on
planes visiting more than a dozen states and 20 cities. I visited the villages
and countryside of America. The land is fertile but poor in scenery compared to the countryside in Britain. I walked on the shores of lakes, and in
America the number of lakes is greater than the lakes created from the

overflow of the sewers in the Arab world. I saw the theaters of Manhattan and the nightclubs. I witnessed drug dealers making a deal, laying their goods on the scale as the customer desires in broad daylight just like normal merchant, even though a police officer was standing on the corner. It was as though we were in Cairo's popular district al-Batiniyya, where drugs are openly sold, and not in New York. I looked at the houses and cemeteries of movie stars in Hollywood. I read a prayer for the spirits of the late Dallas Perry, Edward J. Robinson, Lana Turner, and James Dean.

I saw the lives of the poor; in the district Rabia in Giza, the condition of the poor is better than the poor neighborhoods in America. I realized that there was no room for racial segregation in the poor neighborhoods, because the poor blacks and whites live side by side in peace and tranquility, waiting for God's deliverance. I saw thieves in the night and burglars who steal in broad daylight. I entered bars that offer a drink for three dollars and allow you to view *zalt malt* (stark naked) women dancing in front of mirrors. I felt sad because I had come to America too late in life; I should have visited it 30 years ago. My real problem was that I was unable to complete my visit because of my poor health. I hope that an opportunity for me to visit the United States will present itself again so that I can see the states I did not see and be overwhelmed by the places my eyes never gazed upon.

One piece of advice for the *wika* (cheeky) who plans to visit *Amrika,* chase the idea from your head if your birth certificate indicates that you have passed the age of 30. I tip my hat now and say goodbye to America, tipping it even though I do not own a hat or even hair on my head. But it is the complex of the *khawaga* (western gentleman) that has hit some of us and so we started trying so desperately to resemble the *khawaga* in all his glory and elegance. After all, he who resembles the *khawaga* will be most honored in the end.

I say goodbye to America as I prepare to take the plane to return home. It is from the depths of my heart that I take my last look at America . . . Bye-bye, country of Uncle Sam . . . Bye-bye, country of the rough and tough, greedy and needy, wealthy and healthy, revolutionary minds and organized crimes . . . Bye-bye, land of dreams.

—Translated by May Kassem

26.

My Story with Eva [Ivana Trump] (1993)

ALI SALEM is one of Egypt's most famous playwrights. His plays are primarily political satires on bureaucracy, corruption, and tyranny. We see this in *The Buffet* (1967 or 1968), a rather gloomy Kafkaesque work about being a writer under a totalitarian regime and in *B.A. in Ruling the Masses* (1979), in which Salem aims his telling blows at autocratic regimes with his sardonic style. His 1993 satirical work, *My Story with Eva [Ivana Trump]*, tells of an imaginary relationship with the beautiful divorcée of the famous American millionaire, Donald Trump.

I was going to keep my marriage to Ivana Trump a secret forever. But because of the gossip and all the lies that were published about me in the Western press—lies that were meant to smear my reputation—I had no choice but to speak out, especially when it was rumored that it was I who spoiled the relationship between Ivana and her ex, the millionaire Mr. Trump who, I must say, is a fine man for he never said a bad word about me or her.

. . .

I didn't have much to do that night so I accepted Mrs. Ivana Trump's invitation to her party. What I expected was to meet one of those obnoxious, filthy rich millionaire type ladies; the type that would only talk about money and figures. What I didn't expect was that that night would become a turning point in my life.

In her gorgeous, spacious garden Mrs. Trump received us. Do you remember how Audrey Hepburn used to look when she was young? Well, let me put it another way. Do your remember Elizabeth Taylor's beauty some 40 years ago? Well, add to it the beauty of Susan Heyworth, Suad Husni, and the rest of Egypt's beautiful ladies, and if you mix all of this in a blender, adding some rosewater and all the world's honey and whipped cream, you will end up with Ivana Trump! She is like a good-scented apple tree whose fruit is dollars. She has a smile that summed up all the known charm and beauty of her native Hungary. As for the gracefulness with which she was moving about, no words in the world's dictionaries can fully describe it.

"Ali Salem, a playwright from Egypt," this is how my friend Yihya introduced me to her.

"Oh, Egypt! The pyramids, the Sphinx, Sadat, Naguib Mahfouz . . . you are most welcome here," said she.

When Ivana talks she forces you to listen to her, not because she has such a powerful presence but because of the wonderful music of her speech. For a while we were busy with eating and drinking and talking about the Middle East crises. Suddenly Ivana came close to me and said in a friendly tone, "So how's my Egyptian friend doing? Is everything all right?"

"My lady, I thank you for your hospitality. Indeed, my lady, everything is all right, even better than all right. I also thank you for kindly calling me 'my Egyptian friend.' This is the first time I am called 'friend' by a millionaire lady of your beauty," I said to her with extreme politeness.

"Do you see in me a millionaire lady or a terrific housewife?" she asked laughingly.

"Terrific is not enough, my lady; it does not fully describe you. I thank God for not being your husband," I said.

"Why?" she asked looking upset.

At that moment someone called her and she replied, "O.K., Danny" (that was Danny Quayle, the American vice president).

. . .

[Ivana had asked Ali to be her consultant for a big project that would build theaters in the Middle East. Ali is suspicious of her motives. Here he discusses the issue with his Egyptian friend.]

"Do you believe that Ivana is really in need of a theater consultant and that she plans to build mobile theaters in the Middle East?"

"Under these circumstances one can't say for sure what motive she has," said my friend. "Most probably she, as a very successful businesswoman, just wants to make use of your expertise as a playwright in running her project. Or she, as I personally believe, is actually in love with you."

"What? She's in love with *me?* What do I have to entice a woman like her to fall in love with me? Don't forget she's 43 and I am 56 years old, and I, my dear friend, do not have the looks of Robert Redford or even Jack Palance," I said.

"Cupid shoots his arrows blindly, don't forget," said my friend. "We've never heard that Cupid checks people's birth certificates first before shooting his arrows."

"My dear friend Yihya, you are making fun of me; you're being sarcastic," I said.

"I'm not. It would not be right to satirize a satirist writer. I said what I said because I watched Ivana all evening gazing at you. She must have seen something in you that attracted her attention," he said.

"I know; it's my bald head," I said to my friend and we both burst out laughing.

"But seriously," said my friend. "Be careful and always pleasant in dealing with her. She's no ordinary American. If you cross her, this may reflect on America's behavior in the whole Middle East region. Before you allow yourself to cross her, think about the fate of millions of people in the region," my friend warned.

"I don't have to have adventures of this kind. Tomorrow when she comes to my hotel to pick me up she will not find me. I will leave very early in the morning." I said calmly.

"So you're this kind of person who doesn't welcome lady luck when she comes knocking on his door. There's nothing you should be afraid of; there's nothing to lose," said my friend.

"Oh yes, there's my reputation," said I.

"Your reputation? What do you think she is, a woman from the street? Is she asking you to do something immoral? Or are you this kind of person who shuns good luck when it comes to him? Listen, at 11 o'clock sharp you will be ready in front of the hotel entrance. Don't wear this kind of cheap Egyptian cologne; I will give you a better kind," my friend said.

. . .

[Before meeting Ivana, Ali had met first with his Egyptian friend who advised him to notify the Egyptian embassy in Washington should he, Ali, disappear or be harmed by Ivana. Here Ali elaborates on his suspicion of Ivana's motives in employing him as a theater consultant.]

"Listen, my friend. I am supposed to be with Ivana until tomorrow morning. I will remain incommunicado; this is what Ivana told me on the phone a moment ago. I will give you the private phone numbers of our Egyptian cultural attaché and of our ambassador to the United States so if I don't return by 7 A.M. tomorrow morning you should notify them immediately," I said to my friend.

"You're making a big deal out of this thing," my friend said.

"My dear Yihya, the West wouldn't hesitate to do anything in its struggle against the [Middle] East. Let's be honest; I am an Egyptian creative writer, that's to say I am counted as one of the enlightening elite in the region so if they rid the region of me they rid it of one of its enlightening and progressive elements," I said.

"Well, I agree with you. Let's suppose that they managed to rid the region of you in order to weaken the region then attack it, what can the Egyptian embassy in Washington do in this case?"

"The embassy can always sue for a massive compensation for my family and for Egypt, demanding that the United States forgive at least part of our multibillion dollar debt to it," I said.

. . .

[Meeting Ivana in her LA mansion]

By the swimming pool, Ivana was waiting for me. She was sitting at the breakfast table and several bodyguards were around toting their machine guns. She greeted me in a friendly manner. Suddenly she became angry and shouted in my face, "What is this cologne you have on you? What happened to the cologne you had on yesterday?"

"Did you like the Egyptian cologne? My friend gave me another kind of cologne as a gift," I said.

"This cologne stinks! It was the reason why I divorced my husband. How can you possibly stand to smell this shit?" she said that then yelled at the bodyguards, "Take him to the bath; call an expert on the removal of body odors. Call the manager of his hotel and order him to bring in person the Egyptian cologne from his room. Take his measures and make new clothes for him. The ones he's wearing now burn them immediately," she said.

I was not able to resist the onslaught of about five of her horse-size guards, who jumped on me and dragged me away as Ivana was looking on, laughing and enjoying the scene.

—Translated by Kamal Abdel-Malek

27.

"The Sabeel in America" (1999)

KAMAL ABDEL-MALEK is a native of Egypt who has lived in the United States and Canada for several years. Currently, he is Associate Professor of Arabic and Islamic Studies in the Department of Comparative Literature, Religion, and Film & Media Studies at the University of Alberta, Canada. He also taught at Brown University and Princeton University and is the author of numerous books and articles on popular and canonical Arabic literature.

I met Sheikh Mustapha last summer in Providence, R.I. Before he decided to leave Egypt and settle in the United States, he had got my address from my father, may Allah have mercy on his beloved soul. Wherever he went, Sheikh Mustapha wore his jellaba and carried a briefcase with the Quran and a colorful prayer mat in it. He had the habit of adjusting his thick glasses, which often slid down his big, kind nose. Even in America, he never missed praying to Allah five times everyday. Since I met him he had repeatedly mentioned to me his desire to do something good, an act of benevolence, something for the sake of Allah.

Finally, Sheikh Mustapha thought of something. Excited, he called me up.

"Hello, Ustaadh Ahmad?"

"Yes, who's calling?"

"Sheikh Mustapha speaking. How are you Ustaadh?"

"Thanks be to Allah, Sheikh."

"I thought of something to do for the sake of Allah."

"What is it Sheikh?"

"I want, if Allah wills, to set up *sabeel*, water jars for thirsty passers-by, as an act of charity, the way we do it in Egypt."

"Where would you set it up?"

"The Kennedy Plaza, in front of the city hall building. It will serve many thirsty people, especially Brown University students, they like to drink, you know."

"Good act of charity, Sheikh. It may cost you some money, though."

"Have faith in Allah, Ustaadh. He will provide."

Sheikh Mustapha asked me to help him and I promptly agreed. The first thing to do was to obtain a permit to set up the *sabeel*. Since I did not know how or where to obtain such a permit, I took Sheikh Mustapha and we went to Mayor Buddy Cianci's office. Buddy Cianci smiled broadly and told us that it was the first time such a request had ever been made in the entire history of the state of Rhode Island. He then advised us to go to the Department of Public Health and to the local police station for the necessary permits.

As I mentioned before, the Sheikh explained to me that he wanted to set up the *sabeel* in middle of the Kennedy Plaza; in this way it would serve the crowds of people in the many office buildings, Brown University, and Rhode Island School of Design. He said that he would like to go every morning to fill the water jars himself and repeat the name of Allah as the water poured into the jars. We would need someone, he said, to tend the *sabeel,* so he asked me to put an ad in *The Providence Journal-Bulletin* for a "*sabeel*-tender, no experience necessary." I did.

At the Department of Public Health, Mr. Joe Fraticelli, the director general, raised his eyebrows as Sheikh Mustapha, through my interpretation, explained his *sabeel* project.

"Why don't you invest your money in something else, Sheikh?" Mr. Fraticelli asked.

"Invest? I am doing this for the sake of Allah, good sir."

It was agreed that a health inspector would go every week to check the hygienic conditions of the *sabeel*. Sheikh Mustapha did not hesitate to pay the inspection fees.

To register the project at city hall was not an easy task. Should the *sabeel* be considered a nonprofit enterprise? Could the Sheikh claim the expenses paid to finance the project as tax-deductible?

These issues sharply divided the city hall officials. The difficulty of settling the matter arose from lack of precedent. The *sabeel* project was the first of its kind in the entire history of Providence city hall. A clever official suggested that a committee of five officers and an English-Arabic/Arabic-English interpreter be dispatched to Cairo to study the case. It turned out that the Egyptian government did not keep records of *sabeel* cases since Egyptians never had to register their *sabeels* in the first place. However after a whole month of fact-finding missions, several sessions of committees and subcommittees with their arguments and counter-arguments, the sheikh was granted a *sabeel* permit.

By now the procedure of setting up the *sabeel* was almost completed. Three *sabeel*-tenders were hired, in addition to two licensed *sabeel*-bouncers, and a health inspector. We also obtained all the necessary permits from the Providence city hall, the IRS, the Providence Police Department, plus a good letter of recommendation from Mr. Joe Fraticelli, the director general of the Department of Public Health. Furthermore, an office overlooking the city hall was rented since it was necessary to hire an operator, a secretary, a computer expert to maintain the "Sabeel Web Page," (www.sabeel.com) and of course a manager to supervise the *sabeel*-tenders.

The inauguration day was a remarkable event. Newsmen, radio and TV reporters poured into the Kennedy Plaza. Rhode Islanders received the *sabeel* news with much enthusiasm. Huge amounts of water were consumed that day. A few days later, the necessity to expand became apparent. Sheikh Mustapha had to add more water jars and employ more people. He was advised to hang the typical American sign "NO LOITERING" in front of the water jars. (The sheikh was amazed at American legal restrictions on loitering, pointing out that while we in Egypt are deprived of some fundamental rights, we at least have the total freedom to loiter anywhere we want. Isn't it puzzling, he said to me, that in the very democratic America, people can call their president names, denounce their government, have nude beaches, and carry guns, but cannot loiter?)

Like fire in dry grass, the news of the *sabeel* traveled all over Rhode Island. Sensational headlines such as "ARAB WATER SHEIKS FLOOD OUR STATE," "WATER FAUCETS, ARAB STYLE, STUN RI SHOPPERS," appeared in the local newspaper. *Time* magazine ran a special issue on "THE SPREAD OF ARAB-FUNDED HYDRAULIC PROJECTS IN NEW ENGLAND." Fashion magazines like *Cosmopolitan* promoted the water jar as the new sexy shape, and heavy-bottomed American young ladies with small bosoms were just delighted, at long last, they wrote in their letters to the editor, America admitted that our water jar shape was now sexy. Not to be outdone, *Mademoiselle* magazine figured a picture of an upside-down water jar as the sexy shape, and young women with big bosoms and lean bottoms hailed the new shape as *the* ideal shape for the millennium. (Supporters of both groups of women are rumored to be scheduled to battle out their differences on a future *Jerry Springer* show, so check it out!). Jane Fonda took advantage of that fuss about the *sabeel* water jars and produced a new video, "Arabic Aerobics with Jane Fonda."

For weeks on end the mass media inundated the airwaves with sensational news of the *sabeel* business, so much so that a local Zionist organization expressed its alarm at what it termed blatant Arab meddling in American internal affairs. In a matter of days, a fully-annotated study under the title, *S.I.P. Matters,* was published (S.I.P. stands for the Sabeel in Providence) providing watertight arguments that the whole *sabeel* tradition had in fact been established centuries ago not by the Arabs but by the ancient Israelites (several prominent American writers with Zionist sympathies endorsed the book). A comparatively literate professor (rumored to be a graduate of the department of comparative literature at Brown University, but Allah knows best what the truth is) delivered a lecture entitled, "Sabeelolgy: Allusions, Delusions, Fusions and/or [Con]fusions: Comparative Perspectives Gleaned from World Literatures with a Special Omission of Any Reference Whatsoever to Arabic Literature" in which he argued that, curiously enough, many allusions to the *sabeel* were to be found not in Arabic literature, as one would assume, but rather in Finnish literature. He did not elaborate. His audience was left a little confused but greatly amused.

Some American companies contacted Sheikh Mustapha and suggested marketing the *sabeel* water jars as a new American drink à la Coca-Cola. They added that they could market also a diet brand.

Of course Sheikh Mustapha never wanted such high-profile publicity. When I dropped in to see him, he looked rather upset.

"I made up my mind, Ustaadh," he said.

"To do what?" I asked.

"I am going back to Egypt," he snapped.

"I understand you are upset but—"

"But what? All I wanted was to do something good, something for the sake of Allah and look what happened, look!"

He pointed to a pile of papers on a table nearby.

"You see these are application forms, invoices, receipts, IRS 1040 forms, separation slips, permits, ledgers, and more and more."

Tears welled up in the sheikh's eyes. I tried to say something but he interrupted me again.

"Allah knows my heart's intentions. I only wanted to set up a small *sabeel* charity to serve thirsty passers-by and please Allah. Instead I find myself running a whole corporation called, 'The American-Arab Sabeel Company, Ltd.' What have I done wrong?"

Three days after our meeting, Sheikh Mustapha left for Egypt.

That year, not a single drop of rain fell on Providence.

VI

Colonial Spanish America in the
Eyes of a Seventeenth-Century Arab (1668)

28.

The Gold and the Tempest:
The Journey of Elias al-Musili to America,
The First Arab Journey to the New World

Written in 1675, this is the account of Father Elias al-Musili, a priest of the Chaldean Church, regarded as the first Arab traveler to the Americas. The trip was supported by the Spanish monarch and the pope. Father Elias made the long journey in order to collect donations for the repair of his church in Mesopotamia. His journey to the New World took place when the search was apace for gold and there was a focus on the building of new settlements in the new continent. The forced conversion to Christianity and the harsh measures taken by the Inquisition against Native Americans went unabated. Father Elias witnessed the deleterious effects of all of these practices and had much to say about them. The Arabic account was rediscovered in Syria in 1905 by Father Antoine Rabbat, the late editor of the Arabic journal Al-Mashriq *(The Orient), who published it in a serialized form the same year.*

Around this mountain I saw straight branches of a plant that bore no leaves and each branch bore three buds (jawzat) which looked like cotton buds; each one of them, when opened, you could see inside it a white dove with its wings, feet; red beak and black eyes. This plant is locally called the "Rose of the Holy Spirit." Many of the Spanish overlords here tried to transplant it in the mother country (Spain) but failed to make it sprout.

. . .

I was told about an Indian native who had a mine rich with silver. The man kept the matter secret and did not inform the Spaniards about it. So he used to go to the mine along with his son and they both would cut away silver nuggets and would carry them home to melt and purify by fire. When I was told that this Indian during the mass donated a large amount of money (40,000 piaster pieces) I sent someone to seek him out. When he came to my house I asked him "Why do you continue to keep this matter as a secret and not tell the authorities about it? The King may grant you money and confer honors on you and your children." He answered by saying to me "I know of Indians before me who revealed to the Spaniards news about similar matters (discovering mines of precious stones) and who then were tortured to death by these Spaniards. This is why." I believed him since I witnessed the cruelties Spaniards committed against the native Indians.

VII

Early Egyptian Travelers in America:
Muhammad Ali Pasha's Trip in 1912

A Passage to America (1912)

PRINCE MUHAMMAD ALI PASHA *(1875–1955) is the son of Muhammad Tawfiq, the son of Khedive Ismail, the grandson of Muhammad Ali, the founder of modern Egypt. The prince received his first schooling in Cairo then moved on to Switzerland to pursue his education. He was fluent in French, English, and Ottoman Turkish, in addition to Arabic, his Native tongue. He became the crown-prince during King Faruq's reign, and after the Egyptian revolution of 1952 he moved to Switzerland where he lived until his death in 1955. He was buried in Cairo. Prince Muhammad Ali Pasha of Egypt sailed to America on May 1, 1912—a mere fortnight after the tragic sinking of the famous Titanic. His stay in America lasted for two and a half months. The prince traveled to New York and Alaska and briefly visited the gold mines, farms, and villages of Native Americans. In order to avoid the annoying curiosities and intrusive questions of the reporters and detectives, the prince went around the country under the pseudonym "Rustum." The prince's account of his journey to America assumes a historical value since it may be the first by an Egyptian traveler to America, as it took place after the one by the Iraqi-born Father Ilyas al-Musili in 1668 and the Lebanese-born Mikhail Asad Rustum in 1894. The account is full of details about many aspects of American life at the turn of the twentieth century. We read about the crowded streets of New York; the poor neighborhoods of the Jewish residents of New York (he calls them "Israelites"); the sheer beauty of Niagara Falls; the sight of wild buffalo; the independence of American women, many of them, he says, were beautiful and wealthy; the shocking racism of white Americans who hoarded national wealth and subjected their natives to a life of abject poverty. The account also includes the conditions of Syrian immigrants and the prince's reminding them that their homeland in the East needed their talents.*

New York: The Noisy City

Time passed and I didn't have any rest in this city. It was three o'clock when the telephone rang and a caller informed me that a car was waiting for us. We hurried downstairs by the *ascenseur* (elevator) which I need to describe here so that the reader may appreciate the kind of trouble we had to undertake. This *ascenseur* thing goes up and down with such astonishing speed that it boggles the mind and unnerves you for it goes up and down in one swoop in such a manner that it would make you loose your balance. Imagine having to take this thing several times in a row.

The car took us to Cook Travel which is on Broadway; it is the longest avenue in all of New York for it is 13 kilometers long. At Cook Travel we were promised a guide that would take us on a tour of the city.

I am one of those people who love peace and quiet, and appreciate the beauty of nature. City life with its bustling and noise does not appeal to me. That's why I grew tired of New York. In this American city I felt as though I had been placed in a hollow cylinder along with pieces of metal and thrown down a slope, finding myself turning unstoppably.

We returned from Cook Travel and went to Central Park through the avenue number 5 (Fifth Avenue). It is the most beautiful avenue in New York, full of great and opulent stores. Much like Hyde Park of London, Central Park is in the middle of the city. We moved on to the Hudson River and I delighted in seeing many of the tall buildings along its banks. After a 4-kilometer ride I saw the statue of General Grant and we continued on to Washington Park which overlooked a school for the blind, the mute and the deaf. As for the bridges on the way, these were truly magnificent in every way—their height and breadth and their astounding engineering. The best of these bridges is definitely the Washington Bridge. We also saw many buildings and schools and universities. We were struck by the sheer size of American universities, their location, and their beautiful look. However, one would not be surprised if one is reminded that America is the country of billionaires. It is common knowledge that America's wealthy men have a jealous and a competitive nature and love to donate generously to scientific and academic institutions. In comparison to their counterparts in Europe, American universities are quite young, so in order to make up for this Americans acquire for their own the best and most beneficial aspects of [European] universities. In this way their universities may end up being of a much higher standard than any of their European or other models. Money talks and with their excessive funds Americans are able to attract to their shores the cream of professors and the most prominent inventors in the world. Americans offer generous and attractive salaries to the studious and the competent and this in turn handsomely pays off.

We returned to the hotel in the evening, so happy with what we had seen during our tour. As a major metropolis New York must have robbers and thieves and criminals, yet much to our surprise we saw so few police-men in its streets and alleyways . . .

. . .

What really amazed me was the sight of many American women who were driving small cars, run on electricity. These women drove the cars; there were no chauffeurs. They were bold and energetic. So I said to my-self: these Americans who have mothers such as these brave, energetic, fear-less, and dynamic ladies, are worthy of their reputation of their outstanding status in the world. Most of what children learn of manners and habits are derived from the mother, for nations rise and fall according to the status of women therein . . .

Before we arrived in this town we had seen those [American] Indians and we now recognized them by their special facial features despite the fact that they replaced their native clothes with European ones. Their features and color bespoke of their race and origin. As for their women they put on veils and that was the reason they stood out in a crowd. The disease-in-fested marchlands in which Native Americans lived had a devastating ef-fect on their health and decimated their populations. As for their lands, these were not properly cultivated. Due to the Native Americans' poverty, they still used outmoded agricultural tools and as a result it was with much pain and exertion that they would harvest what they had sewn.

VIII

Accounts of Arab Travelers to America
between 1996 and 2000

The First Glimpse of New York (1996)

HISHAM AL-HADIDI *is an Egyptian surgeon who traveled to America in 1992 for training at the Dallas Hospital for plastic surgery. The account includes his observations about American society and culture, American blacks, American economy and wealth, the Rockefellers, the Pepsi Cola legacy, foreign policy in the Middle East, the American presidency, the computer in America, corruption in America, the space research, Marilyn Monroe, the CNN, and so on.*

[Author arrived in the JFK Airport in New York]

The first I met were black Americans. I immediately was reminded of all the things I read about them, their problems and their complexes, and of course, the TV series, "Roots" by Alex Hailey. One of them, a black woman, motioned for us to go right if going to New York, and left if going to San Francisco. I queued along with others going to New York and found myself in a large hall with about a thousand passenger served by about ten immigration officers. Half an hour later I found myself in front of one of them who asked me the same questions I had been asked at the American embassy in Cairo. He wanted to know if I was going to be paid by the host hospital or not. When I said "No" he asked me if I had acquired the equivalency certificate for my Egyptian medical diploma. I said "No." He was satisfied with my replies and he stamped my passport with a residency stamp valid for three months with multiple entries. In moments I was in the street outside the airport. I wanted to leave some of my heavy luggage in the airport lockers so I asked Americans, both whites and blacks, to point me to the lockers but none gave me a direct answer. Without exceptions all replied with: "Open your eyes, take care of your stuff, it may be stolen in a second." So I realized that there was no use depositing my luggage since there was no guarantee they'd be secured. When I inquired about the address of a youth hostel or a cheap hotel, I realized what I had suspected all along: Americans and Egyptians speak different languages! I don't understand Americans when they speak their brand of English and they in turn don't get a word I am saying. When Americans speak, their words come from their throats, their sounds are laryngeal where me and my fellow Egyptian when we speak English our sounds are frontal; it is with our lips that we speak. They use slang and American expressions and idioms which are totally different from the ones our Egyptian instructor taught us.

[Author witnessed a demonstration by Black Americans and has this to say]

In the train from the airport a group of young black Americans surrounded us shouting, "No justice, no peace!" I panicked and was relieved when the train came to a stop and more passengers poured in . . . the reason behind this agitation was apparently the up-rise by blacks in LA at the time [May 1992].

. . .

[Street life in New York City]

I began to walk all alone on Fifth Avenue. I couldn't believe myself, I am walking in New York and brushing against real Americans . . . yes, I am brushing against them, no, I should say that I am running into them. Yes, running into rather than brushing against because they are stepping lively and I am walking so slowly, sauntering really . . . on each side of the avenue there are very tall buildings, very modern buildings, very huge buildings, but totally free of any artistic beauty except some of the statues that are usually placed at the front of these buildings

. . .

Americans have many feasts and huge celebrations and during the first days of my stay here in New York City it was the anniversary of the establishment of the State of Israel. Whole long streets were closed for this celebration; tall New York policemen were standing ready on both sides of the street; and floats were passing one after the other, some by Jewish school pupils. Despite my anger at seeing this celebration of Israel (the Intifada was still on at the time, May 1992), I could not help but enjoy and admire these artistic parades by Jewish children and youth . . ."It is a Hymie town!" said one Romanian colleague in muffled anger. As for the mementos, I still have of these parades, they are two black kippas, the kind that Menachem Begin used to wear in the Knesset. Wind blew them off their bearers and I picked them up and hid them so that their owners would remain without them—that was the least I could do for the Palestine cause!

As for the other celebration I attended, it was the gay parade of 1992. About 80,000 people took part in it, 80,000 deviant men and women (*shawadh min al-jinsayn*). How horrible! Every couple of men and couple of women was either in a hoodless car or on a motorcycle or on foot. Some men took advantage of the celebration and put on makeup with red lipstick and facial powder and artificial eyelashes and thin eyebrows, dressed as they were in women's clothes.

31

An Egyptian in America (1998)

ADIL AHMAD SARKIS *is an Egyptian-born lawyer and journalist. He has published a collection of short stories and a number of social studies on marriage and divorce in Egypt and Bahrain. His travel account details his impressions and observations about life in America after his three-year stay and his subsequent visits later on. Some of the aspects he admires in America are the American education, libraries, and ways of raising children. But he is critical of what he describes as American discrimination against Black and Native Americans. The author cites in his travelogue some intriguing claims: Jews did not build the Egyptian pyramids nor did they contribute to the cultures of Latin or South America; Ancient Egyptians actually crossed the Atlantic from Ireland to the Gulf of Mexico; strong relations existed between Ancient Egyptians and Native Americans and this explains why the latter still worship Amon Ra, one of the gods of ancient Egypt; the role of Coptic monks in revitalizing Irish culture; St. Patrick is a Coptic Christian saint, and so on.*

The first clash happened a few weeks after my arrival. I was having lunch in one of the university's restaurants when I first saw a girl who was working in the restaurant heading toward me, and when she came close to me I saw that she was trying to pick up a piece of paper on the floor. When I was about to grab the paper, she confronted me with a furious look and yelled at me. I did not understand a word of what she was saying. What I realized was that she was upset because I picked up the paper. I did not answer back because she left. I asked, Diane, her friend, why was that girl upset with me, and Diane said "because you had stopped her from doing her job when you picked up that paper instead of her." Surprised, I said that I didn't mean that at all. Then she asked why I did that and I replied, "I am Egyptian and it's our traditions to respect women so she doesn't have to bend over." Diane smiled saying that women in Egypt were lucky.

The third time was after the debate that took place between Presidents Gerald Ford and Jimmy Carter who were running for president in 1976. One of the students asked me to set a meeting with her to discuss some topics that would rise during the debate as a non American for her project. I asked her if she was committed in a relationship only to know if this would affect our meeting, so she replied in a low voice that she isn't. I said immediately that it is better. Suddenly, she was upset that I said that, because it was a sensitive topic for her. The girl was originally from Holland with such a beautiful face, but she was a bit chubby, too chubby for American taste at the time—for what was fashionable then was for the girl to look boney and not feminine. Therefore, I started complementing her beautiful figure. I told her if she went to Egypt so many men would find her attractive, so she started smiling again.

In America, a person always has to compliment women over their beauty and style, not doing this is deemed inappropriate. It is exactly the opposite in Egypt and other Arab countries because this would be a form of unwanted flirtation which is punishable by law (strange that it is punishable by law when in our Arab culture there are many poems celebrating the beauty of women).

. . .

Dr. Susan Al-Shami, the wife of a friend Dr. Hasan Al-Shami, a professor of Folklore at the Indiana University complained once to me that when she once gave a gift to an Egyptian lady, she expected the Egyptian lady to open the gift and tell her what she thinks of it. Instead the lady only thanked her without opening the gift. In America a person is expected to open the gift offered and to thank the presenter for it. I had to explain to Dr. Susan that the Egyptian lady meant no offense; she only acted upon Egyptian traditions . . .

The first piece of advice that Dr. Farouk Abdel Wahab [an Egyptian professor at the University of Chicago] gave me was to forget about our Egyptian customs of hugging and kissing men on the cheek or walk hand-in-hand with other males. The second piece of advice was to pay attention to the women in the group we meet.

. . .

A beautiful girl was sitting directly in front of me. I caught a glimpse of a golden chain around her neck with the Star of David. The beautiful girl came to me and asked:

"Why do you hate Jews?"

"Who said that we hate Jews? We are Muslims and to be so we must believe in the great three prophets and their messages: Moses and the Jewish teachings, Jesus Christ and the teachings of Christianity, and the Prophet Muhammad peace be upon him and the Islamic teachings."

She asked me:

"Why do you fight the Jews in Israel?"

"We do not fight Jews because of their Judaism. We fight Israel not because it is a Jewish state but because it is a state that took over Palestine and made its Arab people refugees. They have done and continued to do as what Hitler did earlier with Jews in Europe. We all opposed his actions, likewise we do not accept that the Palestinians be treated the same kind of treatment."

She said: "Don't the Jews have the same right to pursue self-determination? Don't they have the right to establish their own country?"

I said: "We may note that the Palestine problem did not arise until after the Second World War. Large numbers of European Jews migrated to Palestine and wanted to establish their state on its land. Prior to all of this and for many years the people of Palestine, Jews, Christians, and Muslims, used to live together in peace and cooperation as they used to do elsewhere in other parts of the Arab East."

She turned to me and asked: "Are there any Jews in Egypt?"

I replied: "Who lived in Egypt prior to the tripartite aggression which was attended by England, France and Israel in 1956. Tens of thousands of Egyptian Jews had a hold on almost sixty per cent of business activity in Egypt. They had the rights of Egyptians, including in the elections. The Chief Rabbi of the Jewish community appoints a member of the Senate similar to the Christian Patriarch and Sheikh Al-Azhar. They also had the full freedom of worship as they had their courts for personal status issues."

She asked me: "It was said that the Egyptian government was kicking out the Jews from Egypt after the war in 1956."

I asked her: "Can the Egyptian government really expel Egyptian citizens from Egypt?" Were the exit visas, given to Egyptian Jews upon their request, an act of expulsion?"

She said: "Of course not."

I went on to say: "I can assure you that the majority of Egyptian Jews had left Egypt under the pressure of one of the Jewish organizations. The pressure was to the extent of threatening to kill those who refused to provide immigration application, once informed of this."

Another student sitting not far from the first one asked: "You mentioned that you, Muslims, believe in Moses and the Jewish teachings, so what purpose did Islam serve then, coming as it has done after Judaism?"

I said: "Three great religions represent three stages in human history such sequence prophesied in the Book of Isaiah."

The beautiful girl with the fine gold chain with the Star of David responded in astonishment asked:

"Really? Do you think that the Torah prophesied the advent of the Prophet Muhammad?"

I said calmly:

"Yes."

She asked me:

"How can that be? Can you explain this to me?"

I replied:

"For my answer to this question to be accurate and complete we would need to meet another day and check the Torah together. So let's meet again."

IX

Accounts of Arab Travelers to America after 9/11

32

One Americano with Mayonnaise, Please (2001)

Echoing the common command at a fast-food joint, "Give me a hamburger with mayonnaise, please," SAMIR AL-JAMAL, an Egyptian-born humorist, chooses this title to ridicule America and to point out the extent to which American ways have penetrated contemporary Egyptian culture. The book is written in an informal manner using much Egyptian slang. The author talks about America and its relationship with the Arabs, the Arab-Israeli conflict, and America's bias in favor of Israel. He squarely puts the blame on America for all Arab crises.

"Leap Frog" is a game where one of the players bends down and another jumps over without touching him, and then they usually alternate positions. I personally could imagine Bush and Blair playing this game with each other. I was watching a TV interview of a British writer who defended Arabs; he argued that the British were the reason for all the crises in the Middle East region because of what they did in the past, particularly when they gave Israeli Jews a big chunk of Arab Palestine. I would add that while we Arabs are giving the Americans and the British so much oil and money for investments, we are getting nothing in return from them. I would also comment that America unashamedly is using its British allies in order to achieve her goals in this region of the world.

When America decided to invade Iraq, it brazenly argued that Saddam had weapons of mass destruction. America lied to the world while it showed concern for world peace. America lied just to invade and occupy Iraq, to steal its petrol and money, and to create a market for American companies. When America invaded Iraq, it couldn't really find any weapons of mass destruction and it stayed over there just stealing Iraqi's oil and resources. At the time of the invasion, America promised the Iraqi people democracy and peace, however, the only thing that Iraqi citizens received was bloodshed, humiliation, and sheer destruction. The American plan is to divide up Iraq into three different countries, to make Iraq weaker than before. America will not be victorious in this war, as long as there are people defending their country and resisting the invaders.

America tends to deceive nations with lies in order to achieve its political goal, which is none other than its control of the whole world. America's reason to make war on Afghanistan was all fabricated; it was a ploy foisted on the world under the deceitful name of the "War on Terrorism." The whole thing is nothing but a play in which Osama Bin Laden is one of the actors.

All these wars that the American military waged, from the Iraq war to Afghanistan, had only one goal which is the protection of Israel by any means necessary. America wants, with its powerful military in the region, wants to confront Iran or any other party that wishes to challenge Israel. Afghanistan is a strategic place since it lies in the middle of Asia; it is as important as Iraq's position in the center of the Middle East. These strategic places were chosen for their oil resources as well. They promised both countries to be liberated from their respective dictatorial rule and to become civilized democratic countries; however, both countries received nothing but destruction, turmoil, and misery.

America controls most of the Arab countries. It does this in many ways: either by intimidating the ruler, in that if he doesn't listen to its demands it would take punitive measures against his country and by measures ranging from trade embargo to military threat, to regime change. Isn't that what America did to Iraq's Saddam? Americans always try to appear to the world as "the good guys" who want nothing but peace and harmony for everyone. They give themselves the right to interfere in your own internal affairs "for your own good." They did just that in Lebanon when they forced the Syrian army to leave Lebanon. Of course, the Americans' real reason was to protect Israel against Syria, Hezbollah and its Iranian allies. Americans put pressures on Lebanon to act against Syria and used some Lebanese politicians to do the job for her. America should really let other countries decide for themselves, freely.

America uses a double standard in everything it does. When an American magazine or newspaper publishes insulting articles on the Quran, they call this freedom of speech, which they would repeat time and again is a fundamental right in America. However, when people talk freely about Jews, Hitler, and the Holocaust this would be considered Anti-Semitism, and the person who writes about that or takes that lightly would be prosecuted and penalized. When it comes to Jews, America suddenly becomes so touchy and everything will be looked at in a different way. While if anything bad happens to Arabs, then it is considered to be the normal result of their behavior.

The American government is trying its best to stop Iran from developing a nuclear weapon. They are constantly trying their best to prevent Iran from acquiring that knowledge, even though Iran only wants the nuclear knowledge for peaceful purposes, like generating cheap energy. When Korea, the country which has a nuclear weapon, states in public that it had nuclear weapons and that it was not scared of the United States of America, America's government does not do much. The reason behind this is that Korea is really far from Israel, but Iran is close to Israel and it poses a threat to Israel's existence. That's the only reason that the American government is fighting against Iran and trying to get the world's support to prevent Iran from becoming a nuclear power.

America and its favorite ally, Israel, are trying to exterminate the Palestinian people. America is giving the political coverage for Israel, while Israel enjoys sending its F-16's to bomb poor and innocent civilians everywhere. They want the people to leave their country and immigrate to other countries so they would have more space to build more Jewish settlements and bring more Jews to Palestine. They are doing that by making it harder for the Palestinian people to live in their own rightful homeland. All of that is happening with a puzzling paralysis in the Arab world with only a few demonstrations demanding to keep Arab rights and dignity.

33.

One Hundred and Eighty Days in Yankeestan (2002)

WAFAA IBRAHIM *is a professor of Philosophy at Ain Shams University in Cairo, and a regular contributor of articles to Al-Ahram, Egypt's national daily. Hers is an account of her trip to America in the summer of 1997; however, the book was published in 2002, a year after the horrendous events of 9/11. It covers topics as varied as women in America, shopping in America, American cultural traits, globalization, metaphysics, and Monica, and ends with a chapter under the telling title: "America, the Siren."*

A few days before I left America, returning to my beloved Egypt, I remembered my meeting with the American consul when I was applying for a visa. He asked me about the purpose of my trip to America and when I said to him that I wanted to discover America, he replied that it was discovered some time ago by Columbus. So I said that Columbus discovered the geographical location but I wanted to discover America not as a fixed location but as a process! The consul gazed at me and said that he knew something about philosophers and that he always admired them because they appear to have a different take on issues.

Before my trip, America for me was a book or a tale told by a visitor. Now America is a panorama of life and varied experiences. But have I managed to discover the real America after a brief stay in places like Philadelphia and New Jersey? Or is it better to say that I tried to understand America and its pragmatic philosophy from a theoretical perspective?

. . .

I raised my head up and much to my total surprise I saw America in front of me. She looked like a tall and strong woman with a radiant face and confident pose. Hers was a full figure yet graceful and proportionate, reminding one of those elegant and opulent palaces of yore. She possessed beauty and majesty, lure and awe, inspiring in one fear and attraction all at the same time.

I said to myself: "This is then America, America the Siren! America with its lure and awe, beauty and majesty, enticing and repelling all at once; no matter how strong I am, I cannot escape her control over me. But how can I possibly have a dialogue with America when she is alluring me as she is now? I must swim away from the field of her magnetic power, maintain my own bearings and distance in order that I may have a dialogue with her. "How are you doing, my dear daughter?" came her booming voice. "I have been watching you throughout the past few months, and must say I have come to admire your Egyptian personality, your dynamism, and I understand that you are here to have a dialogue with me and to challenge me. That sounds good to me so let's hear what you have to say."

. . .

I asked America: What are the characteristics of your national personality? Who are you exactly?

America's face beamed with a big smile as she replied—referring to herself in the third person:

"America is unique among nations; for America, the greatness of a nation should not be gauged by the wealth of her past but by the great achievements of her present, the sheer power of her position in the world, her ability to stand on her own, to control world events and to spread her hegemony the world over. This has been America's position for decades."

I nodded that I agreed and she went on bragging about her power and hegemony:

"This land, since the time Columbus came to it in 1492, has managed to attract to its shores immigrants with great minds and skills and to prove that the greatness of the place is measured by the greatness of the inhabitants occupying it. If the place is a great one in terms of geographical location and natural resources, it still needs inhabitants capable of realizing its potential and reactivating its inner vitality."

. . .

America continued to brag about her natural and human resources as though she were not part of the world but the whole world, the paradise on earth, innocuous and sinless, secure and fearless. So I found myself asking her: "Were you just a land without people when Columbus discovered you?" She replied: "No, my land was inhabited by what is wrongly known as Red Indians. My aboriginal inhabitants were people of great cultures like the Aztec, the Inca, and Maya."

I said to America: "But Columbus and his followers erased this history and put the Europeans at its center."

America grimaced at my remarks and said with a deep and confident voice: "Origins, my dear, can't be erased or moved aside unless they contain too much weakness and fragility to survive the vicissitudes of time. Native culture, as fair-minded scholars would tell you, was self-centered, preoccupying itself with forms and rites, more so than with establishing links with other cultures, unable to acclimatize to its surroundings and allowing inner divisions and conflict to weaken it, creating apertures through which the Europeans managed to penetrate."

I said: "Was it the duty of the Europeans to wipe out any culture that had difficulty adapting?"

America replied with a challenging tone: "I will reveal to you a devastating secret, don't relate it to your fellow Egyptians! Native Americans could have met the challenges they had faced in this land, but their fundamental mistake was their gullibility, for they believed what the invaders promised them, promises that were not honored. These Natives failed to come up with new ideas and concepts, as Todorov said, with which they could have faced up to the invaders. If people fail to produce new concepts and ways to adapt to the world around them they will go under and suffer a fate similar to that of the American Natives. This is the truth, whether you want to say it to others or not, I don't really care. Your conditions will not improve at any rate!"

I kept silent for some time, stunned by this devastating truth which we keep hearing nowadays all over the world presented to us under the guise of world peace, globalization, and human rights.

America went on to say: "When the European pioneers settled the land and wanted to cultivate it, they found that their own methods ran counter to the dearly held ideas of the Natives which embrace that one need not produce more than one needs. For the pioneers, that meant that the new fertile land would remain under-cultivated, ideas underused, potentials under-activated, and resources untapped. Their pragmatism taught them that ideas are but a blueprint to turn what is potential into what is actual and active. Natives were primitive, totally innocent of such ideas."

"Or savages as Columbus called them when he saw them naked!" I quipped.

America ignored my quip and continued to say: "The pioneers were God-fearing people and they believed their Bible where it says: 'You shall know them by their fruit,' for labor and its results are the quintessence of the believer."

I said inaudibly to myself: "You Americans always think of material results and the words of Christ mean more than that."

34.

Returning to California as a Tourist (2002)

GHAZI ABD AL-RAHMAN AL-QUSAYBI *is a prominent Saudi writer and politician. He is the author of several works of autobiographical nature including his recent* Shaqqat al-Huriyya *(Apartment of Freedom) about his years as a student in Egypt. He was also a student in California and this is the account of his return to California not as a student but as a tourist, hence the title of this account excerpted here.*

In the Claws of the Advertisement Beast

How to escape the claws of the advertisement beast in America? When I was in LA as a student, my roommates and I devised these ways:

- To time our visit to the bathroom with the beginning of every TV ad. (It is said that many people in America do just that and in the city of Chicago sewage system is fuller than average during the TV ads.)
- To do some house work such as washing dishes or pots and pans or taking the garbage bags out.
- To start chatting the minute the ad starts and in this way we behave like the proverbial monkeys: we don't see or hear the ad.

Such were our ways by which we managed to enjoy TV shows and avoid the deleterious effects of TV ads on our sanity.

That was then when I had come to America as a student but now I am here as a tourist with children and a wife and I had to endure the all pervasive ads of the American TV channels. I surrendered myself to the claws of the beast. No escape. As the Arabs would say: if you can't have what you like, you need to like what you have! For this reason I "decided" to enjoy the ads; in fact I ended up watching so many of them during my brief visit in America. I even studied and analyzed these ads and came up with these conclusions:

1. These ads don't really tell you where to find the items you need to consume; they brainwash you so that you end up needing items you never thought you'd need. Examples: who would on his own think about buying the recorded music of some obscure singer who had died sixty years ago? And who would want to buy a book on the history of witches and witchcraft? And who would want to buy a videotape with the title: "The Silliest Shots in the History of Football"?

2. Ads go to an extreme, to an obscene degree, in depicting the shortcoming of the viewers. For example an ad for certain toothpaste would depict your mouth as having an unbearable stink, so stinky it might kill a lion. Another ad for deodorant would tell you that your BO is enough to finish off a Spanish bull if you were to be the matador. Another for a sedative would want to convince you that you are on the brink of a massive nervous breakdown! As for women, the ads would not hesitate to imply that without the makeup items and beauty products they present, a woman would look uglier than Satan's wife, fatter than the grizzly bear, and without certain cleaning products her kitchen would become more stinky than a pig's sty. In this way the ads would want the males amongst the viewers to think that without their products they are stinky, fat slops, nervous, suffering from headache, heartburn, constipation, hemorrhoids. As for the females, the ads would want them to feel that without their products they would continue to be: ugly, disgusting, with revolting BO, totally repulsive to men, and in addition to all of this with lice in their hair and cockroaches in their kitchens. All of this in order to advertise for a certain perfume, a lipstick, an insecticide, etc. Is there a more decent, honest, and honorable way to sell products? I wonder.

3. Ads appear to contradict one another. Ads for beer followed by ones about alcoholism and the special clinics for alcoholics. Others about delicious food urging you to stuff your face with it are followed by ads about dieting, "Slim Fast" and sportswear. Ads that use sex are followed by ones cautioning you against "unsafe sex" (come to think of it the fear of AIDS has caused millions to abstain from sex, a remarkable result that all preachers and reformers and doctors have failed to do in decades.) Pity on the TV viewer in America; he starts off with deficiencies and shortcomings and ends up with a split personality!

Why is it that America has this ad fever? In my humble view, derived from my modest understanding of my readings in psychology and sociology, it is that Americans when compared to all nations the world over are characterized by their strong desire to work on "self-improvement." Try if you wish to find a single American who is satisfied with his lot in life. You would find him on the move all the time searching for new ways to live his life, new hobbies, new clubs to join, a new diet to follow, new income to have. Americans don't seem to think that there is anything that is impossible: if you can walk, you can dance; if you discover the way the stock market works, you can be a millionaire. In America they believe in self-reliance and that you can learn on your own and a book can change your entire life. Everything in America depends on skill and technique and that you can learn, if you like, skills such as swimming, driving, public speaking, management, even how to flirt with women! You can even learn the skill and technique of relaxing.

Books that are for self improvement are bestsellers in America whether the topic is about how to get rid of dandruff or measure your intelligence or interpret your dreams or lose weight in a short time. If the readers are in doubt of what I state here, they should consult the list of bestsellers in America because if they do they will find that many of them start with "How to . . ." (Compare this American restlessness with the kind of totally relaxed laid back ways of our Third World because if you do you will discover one of the secrets of their progress and our regress.)

Ads, of course, exploit this kind of desire to achieve self-improvement. For example:

- Lawyers offer their services to victims of car accidents, promising to get them the highest level of monetary compensation—that is self-improvement money-wise!
- Universities offer short courses for adults—that's self-improvement education-wise!
- Religious institutions urge you to call them up if you care about your inner peace—that's self-improvement religion-wise!
- Sportswear shops selling you sports machines for workout, some of which, hear that, talk to you and call you by your name, urging you to go on with your workout—that's self-improvement aerobic-wise!

I must admit to the readers that I am tempted to publish a book on how to raise camels and make a fortune. I bet you it will be a bestseller in America!

Disneyland, wonderland . . . the first time I visited it I was 22 years old and yet I felt like a little child as I went through it. Here it is the wonderland once more in front of me. It didn't change that much but like all authentically beautiful things in life it grows with confidence, it goes on with fortitude, it lives on and does not grow old. So how come I grew old and it didn't? . . .

We toured Disneyland, this wonderland of the future and its adventures into space. Here is the Cinderella, the poor girl who turned into a happy princess . . . here is the borderline between the civilization of the white man and the primitive ways of the American Native and here is also the sad story of how that very civilization came carrying a bag of mixed gifts, of alcohol and syphilis, and decimated the Red Indian along with his animals.

Suddenly an annoying thought crossed my mind about those Saudis who want to plant overnight a Disneyland in the middle of Riyadh or Dubai or Bahrain. As though Disneyland were some seed of a date tree that you plant wherever you wish (by the way we Saudis now import date tree seeds from America—just great!) Or as though Disneyland were a prefab unit or Lego castle set up in minutes and dismantled in minutes.

Disneyland was a project that took decades in the making and now we want to have a Korean company build it for us in months? Disneyland is a whole magic kingdom run by an army of technicians in every field—so is it our intention to transport it to our land lock, stock and barrel? Moreover would our youngsters recognize references to Mark Twain and Tom Sawyer and Frontiers and Pirates of the Caribbean? Would we be able to come up with our own names and references and make a ship after Ibn Majid the famous sailor and an island after Hayy bin Yaqzan the hero of the great philosophical tale and a land after Alamalek, etc. Only when we are able to do all of that should we set out to build our own Disneyland. For the time being let's leave Disneyland where it belongs; it is not made of metal and concrete; it is part of the living tradition of modern-day America.

35.

Deconstructing America:
9/11 and Its Aftermath (2003)

RIDA HILAL *is an Egyptian journalist who went to America in 1998 to work as a correspondent for a daily. He published the first edition of his book in 1998, the second in 2001, and the third in 2003 with a preface on the 9/11 horrific events. The dedication of this last edition is to New York City "the most beautiful of cities and the richest in art and finance, with my shock and pain for the attacks on her on 9/11."*

When the first edition of my book appeared in 1998 my purpose was to present a detailed picture of America, its culture and society, and politics. In it I tried to deconstruct Americans not just through texts by or on them but also through their own acts, achievements and experiences in exercising their freedom in areas like politics, religion and sex. In the book, I also pose the question about the possibility of the collapse of America as we know it, much like the collapse of the Soviet Union. I conclude by saying that if this possibility is to materialize it would have to be due to internal fissures in the American society, the unraveling of the moral fabric of American life and institutions.

When the second printing appeared in 2001, before the suicidal attacks of 9/11 on New York and Washington, it appeared without any addition to the first edition . . . Some of the reviews of this second printing surmised that those responsible for the attacks might have been violent militias in the U.S. or that America's unraveling was near at hand. But when the third edition appeared in 2003 I had to preface it with a long note on the 9/11 attacks.

The book presents America as a melting pot of diverse ethnicities, cultures, religious traditions and values, such as the belief in personal freedoms, pragmatism and, of course, the American dream. The book shows how America moved from a "promised land" for diverse immigrants to a crusading nation intent on Americanizing the world by force if need be, something that has aroused so much hatred of America the world over. The book shows also how the American dream is being eroded by the strife between the actual and the ideal, poverty and wealth, black and white, money and power, egalitarianism and the special interests of lobbies. The book also sheds light on the relative role of religion and the tension between the religious and secular forces in America, the attempts to Judaize American Christianity and the rise of the Christian Right in America and its wielding power over decision making institutions. The book also deconstructs popular culture in America in order to define American self-image and American attitudes towards the other, be it "The Ugly Arab" or the "Muslim Enemy Combatant." The book concludes that America is vulnerable from within: its melting pot, its values, its dream, its social fabric, etc. by the laxity of the American institutions and the spread of violence, crimes, and the deleterious effects of all of this on the moral and ethical behavior of modern-day America.

The 9/11 attacks on the twin towers and on the Pentagon came to prove that the enemy was within and that America's collapse would be caused by an implosion, not an explosion. The America historian Paul Kennedy said that America as the sole Superpower did not only fail to act as one before 9/11 but that it also failed to protect its own internal front against terror attacks . . . Paul Kennedy was right when he described America as an empire with an Achilles' heel—an expression by which he means the American society from within . . .

The 9/11 terrorist attacks shook the foundations of fundamental American institutions such as the melting pot, religious tolerance, civil liberties, and separation of powers and the idea of "Manifest Destiny" which assumes that the Lord has chosen America to lead the world onto the path of freedom and progress. These were the values that have shaped America to make what it is. If these values were to unravel so would America itself. Samuel Huntington said it: "If the American values were to collapse and be replaced by ethnic and cultural secessionist movements then America as we know it would join the Soviet Union on the dust bin of history."

36.

Dusk in America (2003)

MUHAMMAD AL-JAWWADI *is an Egyptian-born physician. He visited America twice in 1983 and in 1991. His first visit was as a researcher and a panelist in a conference on geriatric issues and modern technology and he later published a chapter about the visit in a travelogue under the title,* Rihlat Shabb Muslim *(The Journeys of Muslim Youngman, 1987). This account was published as the third edition in 2003 and contains the author's descriptions of his life in Cleveland, OH, and his research on heart diseases in a major clinic there, and his friendships with Americans in his city.*

Americans define theirs as a nation that hosts anyone who can contribute to its civilization. When I was there, I was surrounded with generations of Americans who were not even born in America. It is worth noting that America does not belong to the Americans only; it is the home of anyone who is ambitious and industrious. This is the very foundation by which Americans defined their Empire . . . At the same time, America is not the home of all ambitious immigrants or wandering seekers of a refuge, but it is the home of those who excel in the professions and skills that correspond to America's professional demands.

. . .

America's investment in research centers and academic research is beyond my comprehension. Scholars from different disciplines immerse themselves in the endeavor of approaching the same subject matter from different angles . . . The elective subjects that university students in America choose, reflect to a great [extent] their interest. A Muslim professor teaching at one of the American universities once surveyed his students at the end of the semester about the reason behind enrolling in his course. One of the statements by a Jewish female student was: "To fight Islam." It is possible that she was not aware of her professor's creed, but she also might have been indifferent to that.

. . .

Did America really manage to overcome its racial discrimination? Or, is it still in denial? As I was contemplating this question, I have to admit that I was overwhelmed by the contradiction between America's statistical representation and its reality. I am personally tempted to think that 90% of Americas' demographics consist of African Americans. This is contrary to the published figures in which we are led to believe that the majority is white Caucasian Americans . . . Look at busses and hotel lobbies, you will see the dominating presence of African American and other minorities. This is despite that fact that the statistics indicate that they are only 60% of the population of a state like Ohio. It is really hard to believe these statistics. Even with a quick glance at the American TV ads, you will find out that TV stardom may be limited to blacks.

. . .

At last, I would like to point that the Americans have a great sense of congeniality. I encounter this on a daily basis as I walk through the Cleveland hills to the bus stop or to the supermarket. People will nod a greeting to me, even those sitting on their porches. Ironically, they tend to be quite reserved whenever I encounter them at social events.

At the hospital, my colleagues were very eager to ensure that my stay in America was pleasant. They asked me about my residence, my fasting, and my hobbies, and even how I spend my spare time, but not from the first time . . . I definitely want to emphasize that Americans are not like the British, in fact, they are eastern at essence. Maybe they are more eastern than the easterners I know.

37

Would You Like to Hate America? (2003)

Y USUF MAATI *is an Egyptian humorist writer who has published a number of satirical works that deal with social and political issues in modern-day Egypt. He published this book,* Would You Like to Hate America? *as a response to the widely distributed book* Why Do People Hate America?— *written by two British authors immediately after the 9/11 attacks. Maati dedicated his book to Christopher Columbus in this way: "To Christopher Columbus, the adventurer of Jewish descent: your discovery of America has caused us great pain, may the Lord punish you for what you did. Without your discovery I would not have written this book. If I were to ask Columbus: 'How do you feel now that you have discovered America? He would answer: "A big mistake, I am really sorry for that."' The book deals with diverse topics: 9/11 attacks on New York and Washington, DC; American movies; President Clinton and his affair; why I love America.*

Why Do I Love America?

If America were a lady standing in front of me now I would say to her: My lady, who said that I hate you? I may be a shy and a modest person but I really love you, I am passionately in love with you, head over heel. I am totally overwhelmed by your charm and beauty. Ask and I will give you whatever you wish. Such is the case of Arab lovers . . . when we love we are devoted and faithful lovers. We are poets by nature but we are unable to express our true feelings; we don't have the freedom to do so. Why do you judge me so harshly? You lady are powerful and wealthy and you are so harsh with me. You find joy in humiliating me and I don't complain. You force me to sit and negotiate with this despicable creature the end of the Arab-Israeli conflict and I sit and negotiate. You throw crumbs of aid at me then you abstain, then you resume and I don't complain. You have decided for me what to eat and what to drink and what to wear and I don't complain. In fact I have adopted your ways in all its details: I take a hamburger for breakfast, Kentucky Fried Chicken for lunch, I drink Coca Cola, wear the baseball hate backward, leather jacket and tattered jeans. I imitate you and imitation is a form of compliment as they say. What have you done in return? You've interfered more in my affairs and argued that you know what is good for me more than I do. And when you dropped your bombs on our lands, some of us thought that you did that because you wanted to occupy our lands, how stupid! I of all people understood that you did that in order to reshape our region and to rebuild our countries. Even when you dubbed your bombs "mother of bombs" it was such a soothing and motherly label! Mothers have to be tough sometimes when they want to raise good kids, so there's nothing wrong with what you did. You see, my lady America, I was so faithful, so steadfast in my love for you, no amount of bashing can dissuade me from my love for you and my commitment to you. They say that you, America, interfere in our affairs and want to force us to change our school curriculum and I said: so what? Is there on the face of earth a smarter nation than America? They say that you support our enemy, Israel, and I find myself forgiving you. I even defended you saying that you have good intentions and that our common enemy, Israel, is a sly enemy, a deceitful enemy, who may have hoodwinked you, bamboozled you, had you! And that you, innocent girl, may have had to pay for your safety from his harm. You force me to negotiate with this enemy and I do it for your sake. Ok, I will bite the bullet, eat my tongue, and force myself to go to one more negotiation session. What else do you want me to do? You slap me around and I don't say anything. Have you ever seen a lover in all your short history so dedicated as I am? I can bear anything except your charge that I hate you. Lord, no, me hating you? It can't be. His Excellency, the American High Commissioner in Cairo is my master and my lord and he can criticize my articles and my TV series and my books and I welcome his censure and I even delete the parts he doesn't like. I even notify the secret police about fellow-Egyptians who dislike America. For your sake, America, I have become a traitor, spying on my brothers and sisters for your sake. You are my real love. My lady, do what you wish to do to me, throw what bombs you wish to throw on my head but do not ever doubt my love for you and my devotion to you. Me, God forbid, hate America? Never! Remember me, dear America, whenever you watch the sunset. I bear witness that there is no state but the American state and no nation but the American nation, and the Lord is my witness as I utter this testimony of faith.

My lady, here I am your faithful lover and I know that you do not neglect the needs of your lovers and allies. I am waiting for your reward, impatiently waiting. Will you recommend me for a great position, or a prize, by the way any news about the Nobel Prize? Anyway, I leave remuneration to your discretion. As long as I am your agent now I fear nothing and no one. I am yours completely. I am tattooed on your arm. I love you, America, reciprocate my love, let it not be a one-sided unrequited love. Life is give and take and the dollar nowadays, as you know, has become worth seven Egyptian pounds.

38.

Cities of the Wind (2004)

ABD AL-AZIZ AL-MUSALLAM *is an Emirati writer and folklorist. The account includes descriptions of the author's visits to many cities around the world such as Beirut, Amman, Delhi, Cairo, Casablanca, Lisbon, Paris, Atlanta, and Chicago. The importance of this book lies in the fact that it presents an Emirati view of America, something that is rather rare in the midst of so much that has been written about visits to America by Arab writers hailing from other Arab countries, primarily Egypt.*

Atlanta via Chicago (Spring 1995)

My plane arrived in O'Hara airport in Chicago in late afternoon. This airport has a huge sign with welcome phrases in all languages including the Arabic "Ahlan wa Sahlan!" I was given a ride by one America acquaintance who took me first to Libertyville . . .

A while later we arrived at the house of this acquaintance and all I can say about it is that it was a gorgeous house of three levels and four bedrooms. I was exhausted and had to sleep, but in the morning and after breakfast, my host had a whole tour for me. The tour included visits to the museums of science and Lake Chicago.

Four days later I found myself in Atlanta, GA. It is a beautiful city and even though it is a great city to visit you would be surprised to know that Americans do not necessarily regard it a tourist attraction. It does not have beaches or ski resorts and these two are great attractions to tourists, Americans or Europeans. As for Arabs it is indeed a wonderful city to visit.

As for the history of Atlanta you would find traces of it in its streets and monuments since it witnessed some of the events of the Civil War in the 19th century. Some of the historic buildings there include the governor's house, Grant Park House, Martin Luther King district, among others.

39.

Americanli (2004)

SUNALLAH IBRAHIM *is a prominent Egyptian novelist. He is the author of several works of fiction that brazenly delve into the social and political issues of modern Egyptian society. He is the recipient of several awards and prizes that recognize him as a great writer; the most recent of these was the award for best Arabic novel—which he declined to receive from the Egyptian minister of culture as a protest against the Mubarak regime. The novel, excerpted here, is set in San Francisco. The protagonist is an Egyptian professor of History with a temporary appointment in America. The novel blends genres since it at times reads autobiographical, a journal, a history book with copious footnotes about real persons and real sources and real authors, and other times as journalistic reportage.*

Shirley appeared at the door to my office. She wore blue jeans with a tight pullover that pulled up her small breasts and ended at midriff. I noticed that she added an extra layer to her red lipstick that made her full lips more pronounced.

"Are you still looking for the book by Thompson?" she asked me, and I said, "Yes."

"A little bird told me where to find it," she said with a smile.

"Great, buy it for me please and I will give you the money. How much is it?"

I put my hand into my pocket to take out money and she stopped me as she was looking at the open door: "Not now, what if someone saw you now giving me money . . ."

She offered to take me to the bookstore to purchase the book

. . .

When we sat to talk, she said: "I didn't like what you said about the hejab at all. Whatever the excuses for the hejab are, the fact remains that being able to dress less is a form of freedom."

"Would you say that the Hollywood style of nakedness is a form of freedom?"

"This is a different matter," she said.

"No, it is all the same; baring the body for commercial or ideological reasons turns it into a thing."

She passed her finger around the tip of her glass and she said, "I don't know."

She raised her head towards me and added: "Fadia, my classmate, said that you ogle girls in the cafeteria."

40.

Why Do They Hate Us? (2004)

NASIR AL-DIN MUHAMMAD AL-ZAMIL *is a Saudi writer. The title of his book echoes the famous question posed by an American woman who emerged from the wreckage of the twin towers on 9/11. It discusses various issues relating to "American terrorism," the history, ideology, and practices of American militias, the hate-groups in America, crime in America, America's deep commitment to the security of Israel, the America invasion and occupation of Iraq, the capture of Saddam Hussein, among other topics.*

We Arab Muslims have been destined to die and have our homes destroyed on our heads, our age-old cities and culture devastated by none other than America and her war machine. And yet there are those among us who still shout: "Long Live America!" and regard America as the model of democracy, freedom, and human rights.

But such voices have been weakened after the post-9/11 because the U.S. has removed its mask and revealed its truly ugly face. After the events of 9/11, the *Wall Street Journal* conducted a survey of Middle Eastern views on America. The journal wanted to find an answer to President Bush's naïve question: "Why do they hate us; we're good people?" The journal surveyed Middle Easterners who had a vested interest in America; people who were bankers and executives in American companies in the Middle East. Rather than waiting for the survey of opinions, Bush should have asked himself this question. Had he asked himself he would have found out that there was a strong anti-American sentiment in the region because of U.S. policy in favor of Israel and its occupation of Arab lands—in Palestine, Golan Heights, and south Lebanon. At the same time the U.S. would accuse anyone defending his land of being a terrorist—is this the American definition of terrorism? And to top it all, the U.S. invades a sovereign country like Iraq, terrorizing and killing Iraqis and pillaging Iraqi sources and riches, with the use of the state-of-the-art weaponry—lawful and unlawful, smart and not so smart bombs and rockets. This was done in the teeth of opposition from European, Asian, and Arab countries, even some people inside America itself. Was it for the sake of liberating Iraq of its dictator that the U.S. sent a quarter million of its soldiers? America spent billions of dollars in the first phase of the war—was this done for the sake of preserving the Iraqi petrodollars for the Iraqis as a gesture of Yankee hospitality? Let's remember that Saddam was one day an ally of the U.S. It was the U.S. that provided him with weapons in order to get him to wage war on Iran. It was the U.S. that said about Saddam's gassing his people in Halapcha that that was an internal affair. It was the U.S. that apologized to Saddam for the campaign against him in American media after the Halapcha affair.

Here's the America cowboy with the noose in hand, leading the cattle to where he wants. Here's the American pioneer with the self-same logic of yonder years: I kill the other guy therefore I am! Here's America as the loose cannon bombarding the defenseless, absolutely impervious to the pleas from other nations to stop the carnage. Here's America practicing its hobby of merciless killing, aided and abetted in that by International Zionism, and heading to shape the whole Middle East in a new order subservient to the Jewish state.

41

The Rise and Fall of the American Empire (2005)

MANSUR ABD AL-HAKIM *is an Egyptian lawyer and author. His published books to date deal with issues relating to the occult and the end of days with titles such as* Doomsday; Nostradamus and the Jewish Conspiracies; The Secret World Government; Iraq: The Land of Seditions and Prophecies; The Awaited Messiah, The End of Israel Will Be in 2022; New York: The City on Top of the Mountain of Fire, *and so on. In his book* The Rise and Fall of the American Empire, *Mansur Abd al-Hakim argues that America has imperial ambitions and that in order to understand this one has to study its earlier history. America obliterated the communal presence of its native inhabitants, the American Indians, and what the author calls the new Anglo-Saxon imperialism that wants to conquer the world and subject it to its will. The author claims that his book is an attempt to deconstruct the American system and cultural patterns and to show that America is about to disintegrate socially, politically, and culturally.*

From its beginning in the eighteenth century America was characterized as an imperial state bent on exploiting and occupying other countries and nations the world over. After her states became fifty America became a real empire, especially after it had inherited the role of the British Empire in the aftermath of the WWII.

The appearance of the American empire was no surprise since it followed the footsteps of other empires, building its own on pillaging and occupying other people's lands and riches and destroying their culture and heritage. America did that to its Native Americans; the destruction and the pillage are unprecedented in human history . . .

The American genocide of the native Indians was based on the notion that these inhabitants were not humans. In this Americans were very much like Jewish Zionists who occupied Palestine in 1948 . . . It is no wonder then that America supports Israel since both countries annihilated their respective native inhabitants under the slogan: a land with people for a people without a land.

In this book we will try, God willing, to shed light on this America empire, which raises the banner of progress, democracy and sets out to liberate the Third World by annihilating it with phosphorous and cluster bombs as it did to the 112 million of its own natives who are now reduced to only a quarter million.

The destruction of nations is but a natural occurrence in world history for Almighty has caused the fall of many empires in the past. America will not be the last empire to fall as the Quran clearly shows there were many other empires in the world which were doomed for destruction . . . this destruction is inevitable if empires are built on oppression, unbelief, repudiation of God's messengers, spreading corruption in the world, and violating other people's rights. The demise of America is predicted by many economists, because if America wants to remain a superpower it needs about 1.5 billion dollars everyday in order to redress the imbalance in its budget. This is in addition to the sharp decline of education by the year 2020 because of a shortage in teachers . . . Whatever the reasons, America's fall is inevitable.

42

Embrace Condoleezza Rice at
Your Own Risk (2006)

ZUHAYR WASINI *is a TV personality working for the Italian TV station RAI. He has a Ph.D. in literature from the University of Granada, Spain, and teaches Arabic at the University of Rome. He has published many articles in Arab as well as Italian and Spanish newspapers and scholarly journals. He is the author of* The Moroccan Theatre *(1992, in Spanish), and* Qatl al-Arabi *(The Murder of an Arab, 1998). His book, from which this excerpt is taken, deals with his visit to the United States as a journalist covering the occupation of Iraq in 2003 and other matters relating to American-Arab affairs. The book cover features a photograph of Condoleezza Rice in black and white with a horizontal divide of her face: half positive and half negative as though she, like America, the country she represents, has a split personality of good and evil. The blurb on the back says this about her: "finally we met the lady; her face reminds us of our fate . . . whenever we, Arabs, met this lady some calamity would follow soon after our meeting. That's why I cautioned my Arab media colleagues not to be close to her, who knows what would happen next? We have a feeling that this woman loves to inflict pain on Arabs and she seems to enjoy it. When I said to my Arab colleagues: "Why don't we have a dialogue of cultures with this lady, they all ran away for fear for their lives . . ."*

[During the visit to the United States]

I turned to Murad, my Yemeni friend, to tell him this joke about Yemen: "The elders in Yemen got together to discuss ways to get their country out of its poverty and backwardness. A rash young man stood up and suggested that Yemen should declare war on America and provoke the Americans to send their marines to occupy Yemen and in this way the Americans

would run Yemeni affairs and improve the living conditions for all Yeme-
nis. An irate old man asked: "My son, this is all good but what if we won
the war against America?"

Ours is a miserable era . . . a strange and a stupid era that defies all rational analyses. And yet we must confess that we Arabs have won the battle with America, do you know why? Look at the Abu Gharib prison and
the torture there, the Guantanamo and its violations of human rights, the
eavesdropping on the American citizens by the Bush Administration, the
limitations on personal freedoms in the U.S., these and more are nothing
but the result of America's long association with us, Arabs; America has
learnt so much from us.

When we witnessed how rough the American police treated people
lining up to see their president (Bush) in a motorcade with the Chinese
president, blocking roads for hours, detouring traffic, etc., it became very
clear to us that America has learned from our Arab ways and Arab presi-
dential motorcades and the rough ways Arab policemen deal with the cit-
izenry. Do you, dear reader, have any doubt that it was the Arabs who won
the recent war with America?

   . . .

If you were to have seen us playing bowling with some American servicemen you'd know what I mean when I say that Arabs don't really know
how to hate others. It was my first time to go to a place like this—a bowling hall—with the clinking of plates and beer bottles in our ears permeat-
ing a friendly atmosphere amongst people who may have their differences
in the outside.

The America officers we had dinner with yesterday and who were very
solemn and serious-looking army men are now here in the bowling hall
horsing around and joking, drinking and laughing, and totally engrossed in
the art of merrymaking. It was a great night of fun.

Two Arabian young women from the Gulf region were with us. They
excelled at the bowling game, and so did the Lebanese and the Danish
and the Egyptian fellows. Why haven't I learned how to bowl before? It
is a simple but really enjoyable game. If you had seen us, how friendly
we were playing this game, you'd have realized civilized nations don't
make wars against each other. Wars are waged by the least civilized
amongst us, by people with no civilization. Of course if we, Arabs, were
to challenge Americans to a game of bowling we'd be beaten hands
down in this American game, but there would not be any collateral
damage at the end.

The loud music made us forget our differences, differences we did not
shy away from expressing the other night when we had dinner with those
selfsame American officers. This kind of human interaction, with food and

music and game and merrymaking in the background, make one soar over conflicts and tension and strife and war and national interests. It was indeed a beautiful night.

At one point I had a strike, I hit all the targets with one strike of the heavy ball and I found myself making the victory gesture a Spanish matador makes the moment he deals the raging bull a finishing blow. Two American officers of Mexican descent understood my gesture and burst out laughing; the last thing they expected, they later told me, was for them to see an Arab like me imitating the gestures of a Spanish matador. It is a strange global world we are living in, but this may be the beginning of a new beginning for all of us. Two Americans from Mexican descent talking to a Moroccan Arab who is also an Italian citizen about a Spanish game and this is all happening in an American city. The more we talk, Arabs and Americans, the closer we will get to one another. While the world has indeed become a global village, there are individuals who are still calling for a clash of civilization, protectionism, and isolationism and a total repudiation of the other. This and other such stances are based on fear of the future instead of facing it with confidence that our togetherness as humans is preordained and sooner or later we are destined to be one with the other in the melting-pot of humanity . . . I wish Oriana Fallaci were with us in the bowling hall so that she may have realized that all her writings she fed to her Italian readership were racist and unrelated to actual human reality.

I say this because back in Italy where I live and work there were strong anti-Arab and anti-Muslim views expressed in the media after the terrorist attacks of 9/11; racist views I did not see in America, the real victim of these terrorist attacks. The Italians were in this case more royal than the king or as they say in Italian more Catholic than the Pope . . .

. . .

My Arab colleagues and I met with many Americans and I was particularly proud of my fellow Arabs as they were so eloquent in debating Americans and explaining the Arab views on what is happening in our Arab region and our relations with America. The debates took place in several locations one of which was the University of Syracuse where both student and faculty listened to our arguments and were patient even when some of us mounted sharp attacks on America, attacks that must have been so offensive to American patriots. Our American interlocutors were patient and even at times showed sympathy to our Arab views. Bit by bit it became clear to us that Americans are really kind-hearted people, honest and candid people. Some of them were willing to admit guilt and were apologetic about their government's actions. Bit by bit we all realized that the real battle is the one against preconceived ideas and the rejection of strangers without having a chance to know them.

. . .

Every Saturday, members of our Arab group of media people would be distributed as guests of American families. It was usually a dinner and it was a great opportunity to get to know Americans and their ways. So at around 6 o'clock, an American lady came to pick me up along with my Bolognese friend, Merek, and our Egyptian interpreter, Mahmud. The car ride took us through the wide avenues of Syracuse and when we arrived at the house another lady was waiting for us along with two dogs and a cat. The welcome was really warm especially from the two huge dogs that jumped all over Merek. As for me and my Egyptian interpreter we found ourselves hiding behind the two hosting ladies, who understood how we Arab Muslims have a problem with dogs (we believe they are unclean animals).

We sat down to talk with a measure of friendliness and embarrassment: small talk followed by remarks about the weather interspersed with drinks and more conversation. We then moved to the dining room where we had our meal with the two ladies.

Mahmud, the interpreter kept asking me (in Arabic): who do you think acts the "man" in this relationship between our two hostesses? Frankly, I don't care about questions like that or bother to ask what relationship these two have with each other. I think that individuals should be free to choose their particular lifestyle. That's why I cared to hear the two ladies talk about the hardships they face as lesbians in their attempts to live in dignity and be treated with respect . . .

When we went back to our hotel, the news about our dinner with two lesbian Americans had spread like fire in dry grass . . . the Arab mind is incapable of understanding this kind of human relationship and that was abundantly clear to me from the many harsh comments by our Arab media colleagues.

Now whenever I remember this dinner with these two American lesbians, who showed us so much courtesy and hospitality and I would even add nobility of spirit, I want to ask the obvious question: what is the reason that would make anyone judge others by their sexual preferences? What difference does it make what they do in their private life? What is so offensive in their practices in the privacy of their home? I must admit I do not understand.

I believe that real democracy is the one that protects the rights of the dissenting minority and that's why I think that some democracies in the world ought to review its negative stance [on homosexuality]. As for us Arabs, well, I am sorry I don't know what to say; I was talking about democratic nations.

. . .

Whenever we saw one of our Arab media group approach or talk to an American woman we would jokingly say: here's a real dialogue of cultures! Some of us, Arab men, tried to convince these American lasses to change their mind about the stereotypes they had about the Arab man who loses his head in the presence of a blonde beauty. Notice I say "tried" and that's accurate because they failed miserably! For they themselves lost their minds as they were talking to the American blondes. I say, so be it; we Arab men have a weakness towards blonde beauties; who knows maybe this is the way to end wars and strife in the world. Who knows maybe Bin Laden perpetrated all his horrendous acts because of an American blonde who turned him down. This is quite plausible as an explanation since there's no other to make sense of his irrational behavior.

I must admit I saw nothing wrong with us, Arab men, talking to American women, whether they were blondes or brunettes. There was pleasure in talking to them in the midst of tedious conferences and interviews and debates. Conversations with America women may take us to new worlds where the eye contact with them would put an end to all the strife and tension and wars we have been having with America! The most beautiful dialogue is the one with eyes, colluding looks that try to create a better world devoid of strife. We love this kind of dialogue of cultures and we regard it as the most important by any measure.

The problem was that whenever we had serious meetings with American male officials and they happened to talk about "the dialogue of cultures" we would laugh and our American partners would look baffled because they would not understand why. For us "dialogue of cultures" had a very different meaning that is not as innocent as it sounds.

One of the guys in our group—I wouldn't mention his name—hit it off with an American young woman. When she asked him about the wedding ring he was trying to take off, he told her with a straight face that it was customary in his Arab country for all journalists to wear such rings so that the authorities would know where to find them in case of an emergency! The funny thing is that the American young woman believed him. Or maybe she made him think that she believed him in order to carry on with this much touted "dialogue of cultures."

43.

Chicago (2007)

ALAA AL-ASWANI *was born in 1957. A dentist by profession, Al-Aswani is the author of the bestselling novel* The Yacoubian Building *(AUC Press, 2004), which is now published in many foreign-language translations and was recently made a movie. His most recent book is* Friendly Fire.

Chapter One

Many do not know that chicago is not an English word but rather Algonquian, one of several languages that Native Americans spoke. In that language Chicago meant "strong smell." The reason for that designation was that the place occupied by the city today was originally vast fields where the Native Americans grew onions, the strong smell of which gave the place its name.

. . .

The history of cities, like the lives of humans, however, suffers vicissitudes of happiness and pain. Chicago's black day came on Sunday, October 8, 1871. In the west of the city lived Mrs. Catherine O'Leary with her husband, children, one horse, and five cows. That evening Mrs. O'Leary's animals were grazing quietly in the backyard of the house. At around nine o'clock, one of the cows was suddenly bored, so it decided to leave the backyard and go to the back barn, where its curiosity was aroused by a kerosene lamp. It circled around the lamp for a while and stretched its neck to sniff at it, then suddenly it responded to a mysterious desire to give it a strong kick, whereupon the lamp overturned and the kerosene spilled and the floor caught on fire. There was a pile of hay nearby that was ignited, and soon the house burned down, then the neighboring houses also burned down. The wind was strong (as is usual in Chicago), so the fire spread everywhere. Within an hour the whole city was engulfed in flames.

The catastrophe was made even worse by the fact that the firemen were exhausted from staying up the whole previous night putting out another fire that had damaged much of their equipment, which was primitive to begin with. The flames soared in the sky and began to devour the houses of Chicago, which were mostly made of wood. People's loud, anguished cries mixed with the sound of the raging fire as it gutted the city, producing a frightful din, as if it were snarling a curse. The scene was frightening and mythical, like the description of hell in holy Scriptures. The fire raged mercilessly for almost two full days until it was finally extinguished at dawn on Tuesday. The damages were tallied: more than three hundred people killed, a hundred thousand (about one-third of the total population) left homeless. As for monetary damages, they exceeded two hundred million dollars in nineteenth-century monetary values. The catastrophe did not stop there: fire and destruction brought forth total anarchy. Roving gangs of miscreants and criminals, thieves, murderers, addicts, and rapists spread like maggots coming from all over to wreak havoc in the unfortunate city. They began to loot contents of burnt-out houses, stores, banks, and liquor stores. They guzzled liquor on the street and killed whoever crossed their paths. They abducted women to gang-rape them publicly. In the midst of the catastrophe the churches in Chicago organized special masses and prayers to lift the pain and suffering, and all the clergy spoke in a sincere penitent tone about the catastrophe as just punishment from the Lord for the spread of heresy and adultery among the citizens of Chicago. The destruction was so rampant that whoever saw Chicago at that time was certain it was irrevocably lost.

But what happened was contrary to expectations. The enormity of the catastrophe was such that it motivated Chicagoans and gave them courage. A merchant by the name of John Wright, who throughout his life understood only the language of numbers and deals, and who was never known for literary inclinations to eloquence, found himself standing in the midst of dozens of shocked and bereaved citizens milling about after having lost all they had to the fire. Suddenly a mysterious, poetic energy burst forth from him and he improvised a speech that was to become memorable in the history of the city. John Wright held out his arms in front of him and his features hardened in what looked like pain (he was a little drunk), then shouted in a loud, cracked voice, "Courage, men! Chicago did not burn; it entered the fire to get rid of its bad elements and will come out stronger and more beautiful than it has been."

Chapter 30

"Dr. Baker is known for his fanaticism against Muslims, and I, thank God, I am a Muslim proud of my religion. He tried more than once to make fun of Islam in front of me but I was dumbfounded and scolded him, so he decided to take his revenge on me and fabricated this issue," Danana said to his wife Marwa who was sitting in front of him on the sofa. Then he bowed his head, his face looking like that of someone stoically and patiently withstanding unbelievable pain. Marwa, of course, noticed several large gaps in what he was saying, so she said, trying to maintain a neutral smile, "This is a strange story."

" Strange Why ?"Your enemy is your enemy of your religion and God Almighty has said in the Nobel Book: *"Never will the Jews be satisfied with thee, neither the Christians, not till thou followest their religion."*

"But you told me before that Dr. Baker likes Egyptians."

"That's what I thought until his dirty reality revealed itself. You know that I am kindhearted and am easily deceived by people."

"Couldn't it just be a misunderstanding?"

"I tell you he is going to expel me from the department, you tell me it's misunderstanding?" Danana shouted angrily. Marwa kept silent for a moment then asked him, "Whatever are you going to do?"

"I don't know."

"Why don't you go to the investigation hearing and tell them the truth?"

"You think Baker's American colleagues will disbelieve him and believe me?"

He bowed his head then said in a subdued voice, "An injustice has been done t me. But God is great. He sent me Safwat Bey Shakir to help me."

Marwa felt that the conversation was getting into unknown territory filled with hidden possibilities, so she maintained her silence. Danana went on as if talking to himself, "Safwat Bey promised me that he would settle the matter with the educational bureau, and after that, he'll enroll me in another university."

"Thank God."

"Have you seen in your life a kinder and more generous man?"

"Of course!"

"So, I ask you, for God's sake, can I turn down any request by this man?"

Marwa looked at him in silence but he persisted sharply," Answer me."

"What exactly do you want?"

"I want nothing but what's good. We, Marwa, are a couple. We are partners, in good times and bad. Right now I am going through an ordeal.
Safwat Bey has done me a big favor."

"What's that got to do with me?"

Safwat Bey wants you to work with him."

"Me?"

"Yes. He'll appoint you as a secretary in his office."

"But I've never worked as a secretary before."

"It's not that difficult. You're intelligent and you'll catch on quick. If
Safwat Bey wanted he could appoint ten American secretaries. But work
in his office is subject to special consideration."

"I don't understand."

"Whoever works with him will get to see highly classified documents.
He wants you because he trusts you. American and Israeli intelligence will
seek to recruit any secretary working with him to have access to your
country's secrets. Your work with Safwat Bey is a small return to his great
favor, but it is also a patriotic act."

Marwa fell silent again, as if the rush of events had discombobulated her
and made her unable to think.

"What do you think?" Danana asked quickly and looked at her like
someone who had thrown the dice in a backgammon game and was waiting for the result. He had prepared himself to convince her by any means.
She must work with Safwat Shakir. He would urge her, beg her, quarrel
with her, use her father to convince her if need be. He sat before her, ready
for any reaction. Several moments passed, and then she raised her head toward him and said calmly with a mysterious smile on her face, "I accept."

44.

Saudis in America (2007)

TURKI AL-DAKHIL *is a famous Saudi author, journalist, and media person-*
ality who has a regular talk show on the Emirati-based Al-Arabia *Arabic*
channel. His highly rated talk show presents some of the most controversial
topics in the Arab world. In 2009 he was selected the best media personality
and his show as the best talk show. The Arabian Business Magazine *lists*
him among the most influential and famous one hundred Arab personalities
in the world.

Other books by Al-Dakhil include accounts of his travels in Yemen and
Afghanistan. His 2006 humorous book Mudhakkirat Samin Sabiq *(Mem-*
oirs of a Man Who Used to Be Fat) presents a candid description of his prob-
lems with overweight and the strict diet he had to follow. This book is currently
being translated into English by Kamal Abdel-Malek and Mouna El Kahla.

His account, Saudis in America, *deals with different aspects of Amer-*
ican society and culture and the presence of many Gulf Arabs in the United
States.

The American woman in her forties was not attractive but she exhib-
ited a remarkable degree of kindness and good nature. She went out
of her way to help me with my accommodation and study. I left her office
pleased with the smooth way everything was going for me but I must
admit I had nagging doubts as to her motives behind helping me out in
this generous way. I thought that I should really be on my guard and move
away from what we call in our country a *dalakha,* which is the state of
being a naive person, a yokel, a hillbilly of sorts. What kind of repaying
would I have to make in return for this generous attention and help from
this American woman?

For a while I thought that I was the only recipient of this special help and
that yours sincerely was the only beneficiary on her "kindness insurance"
program, the one and only client of this lady in charge of international students at an American University. I even went as far as believing that it was

thanks to my mother's prayers that I was so lucky to receive this kind of help in foreign lands. I still remember Mother's prayers on my behalf: "May Allah bring the good and pious people of this earth to be of help to you and block the evildoers from harming you, Son!"

But the truth be told that much to my surprise I found out that this kindhearted American lady did not single me out for care and attention and that other students, males and females of all nationalities, received similar help from her. I even found out that many of the Gulf Arab students thought they were the only individuals who received help from her. It seems that we Arabs think that the prayers of our wonderful mothers make us the only recipients of grace, forgetting that non-Arabs too have mothers who pray for their well-being.

I think that the reason I kept thinking about the kindheartedness of this American lady in her position as a helper to international students is that we Arabs are not used to seeing people who are so professional in their behavior and so devoted to their jobs and so pleasant in dealing with clients. I am confessing this with a great deal of pain, of course. All I can say is this: the American official in charge of the international students' affairs did what she did out of respect for her job, her career, her sense of responsibility, and this cannot be done without a sufficient fund of human decency.

45.

The Egyptian Occupation of America (2008)

YASIR QANTUSH *is an Egyptian lawyer and humorist writer. His book is an account of an imagined Egyptian occupation of America and all the tragicomic events that have ensued. The main character, Abul-Hasan, is a poor man who dreams that he has become the president of Egypt. Abul-Hasan, now in his capacity as the president and the supreme commander of the armed forces, decides to occupy America as a way to find a solution to Egypt's perennial economic problems. The American president is taken hostage and the United States is forced to let Egypt rule it for a while. The Egyptian occupation reverses so many things in world politics so much so that we see for the first time the Security Council issues resolutions in favor of Arabs and against America, America's nuclear weapons are now monitored by the Third World countries, and so on. Abul-Hasan manages to keep America colonized for three days. This colonial endeavor backfires, and, of course, the dream does not go on for long. Abul-Hasan finds himself waking up to his daily chores of standing in the bread line and rushing to work in order to feed his many children and sharp-tongued wife.*

The Egyptian Occupation of America, a Fantasy:

Abul-Hasan's Identification Card:

Name:	Abul-Hasan Ismail
Occupation:	Professional Dreamer
Age:	Dropped off the records of the official census but you can say he is about seven thousand years and a bit
Number of children:	Ranging between seventy and seventy-five millions (according to the state census)
Blood Type:	Congenial
Place of residence:	Among the first in any bread line in our beloved Egypt
Legal Hobbies:	Joke-trafficking

Scene I

[Abul-Hasan has an argument with his friends about the food shortages in Egypt, especially bread. They are all unhappy about the long bread lines, the bread ration for poor citizens, and the bad quality of the subsidized loaf of bread.]

— Does this make sense? We import wheat from America while we've got the Nile and the most fertile lands.
— My good man, America has got wheat enough to feed the whole world.
— So what's the solution?
— Well, since you're brave enough to think of meeting the minister, you might as well go and meet the President himself and ask him to occupy America and bring us American wheat.
— Yah, we occupy America, we occupy America.

On his way home, Abul-Hasan keeps repeating this sentence. He is absent-mindedly, not paying attention to anybody and not talking to anyone, as if the street were empty of all people except him. "Yah, we occupy America, we occupy America!" These words keep turning in his head

He enters his house, quietly. His wife, Enaam, calls him but he does not reply as if he were a zombie. He enters his bedroom and throws himself on the bed and goes to sleep. He has a dream in which he sees himself as the President of the State of the Poor Folks (Egypt). Glory be to God, He giveth and taketh. Here is the will of God granting him authority to rule, authority that he wouldn't dare imagine possible.

. . .

"Long Live our brave President! Long Live our brave President! Long Live the valiant hero! Long Live Abul-Hasan!"

Abul-Hasan shakes his head with the humbleness of the peacock. He points to them in order to be quiet.

"But how can we occupy America without war? Although warring with Americans is not really that hard, you can see by yourselves what is happening to them in Iraq, I am not willing to sacrifice any poor citizen of our Republic of the Poor Folks. I need a way to occupy America without any loss of life on our side."

Vice President Gamal says: "Mr. President, I have a plan. Do you know, Sir, the National Day for our Republic of the Poor Folks is next month. Every year we throw a great party and we invite rulers and presidents from around the world including, of course, the president of the United States of America . . . After the party, the invited delegates will return to their home countries except the Americans. We will then kidnap the American president and give the United States of America an ultimatum: Allow our brave army to occupy your land or else we will kill your president!"

Ministers nodded with approval and the Vice President continues as he winks at the President:

"As you know, Your Excellency, America values the life of each one of its citizens so imagine how much more will America value the life of its own president? Americans, especially their presidents, are always afraid to die. The American people appreciate their democracy and breathe its pure air. Americans know that if an occupation occurred, this wouldn't change their notions of democracy and principles of freedom. In other words, everything will remain as it is for them."

The plan is well received and approved by everybody and Abul-Hasan starts counting votes. The resolution is unanimously approved.

"We, Abul-Hasan Ismail, President of the Republic, have decided to send a draft resolution on the Egyptian occupation of America to the parliament for approval. We need to receive it no later than thirty days from now. May God help you to succeed in this solemn endeavor.

Signed,
President of the Republic, Abul-Hasan Ismail

. . .

[The American president and his entourage are welcomed by Abul-Hasan. The Egyptian secret servicemen drug the drinks offered the to Americans and in a few minutes they all lie down on their seats totally paralyzed. Abul-Hasan holds a press conference in which he declares that unless America allows the Egyptian army to occupy it, Egypt will execute the American president. The Egyptians eventually occupied America and sent the Occupation Committee to run America; however, some institutions, such as the Congress, remained untouched.]

U.S. recent opinion polls show that most American citizens are not concerned about this Egyptian occupation. After all, the principles of true democratic values are deeply engrained in the Americans. No occupation will affect that or shake their beliefs. Therefore, unaffected by anything, everything will run like clockwork. Since its inception, America has always been governed by strong institutions. The government here consists of individuals who are elected by free and fair electoral process. They diligently supervise the plans and resolutions offered by specialists in all areas starting from space exploration, and even ballet dancing. Every detail is accounted for and subject to specific strategies. Therefore, the dynamics of Americans' life will not be paralyzed by the fear of this occupation.

. . .Now the Minister of Finance was urged to put on his thinking cap and work his brain to find any means to obtain money, as much as possible, even through creating and imposing new taxes. At this stage, pilling up the greens is the top priority.

The First Day of the Egyptian Occupation

The first decision declared by the Occupation Committee pertained to the cultivation of ninety percent of the wheat fields of America and establishing a direct flight route between America and the Ghalaba Republic (Poor Folks) to transfer the wheat stacks. The Congressional Committee objected arguing that such decision would be detrimental to the production of other crops. The committee appealed to the International Court of Justice and the fixed ratio was adjusted to thirty percent of American fertile land.

Ten billion U.S. dollars in compensation was imposed on Ghalaba Republic due to this arbitrary decision that jeopardized the welfare of the American people without the consent of the authorities entrusted with the regulation of such laws. Just as Abul Hassan was informed with this news, he contacted the Occupation Committee and was assured that the news was true. He was beside himself with rage. How can this happen? He only sends them to get the wheat and not ten billion dollars sanctions against his republic.

"This is disastrous!" Abul-Hasan said.

The finance minister answered reassuring him:

"Oh, Mr. President, don't worry. I will take care of this."

"Let us see how you would handle this " . . . WHAT ARE YOU WAITING FOR?"

Appendix

Accounts of Arab Travelers to America Unlisted in Part One

Sinbad in the New World (1984)

HUSAYN FAWZI *was one of the most prominent Egyptian intellectuals of the twentieth century. He was a polymath combining expertise in science, oceanography, music, art appreciation, literature, and journalism. He was truly a Renaissance man. He recorded his account of his trip to America in 1974 under the title of* Sinbad in the New World, *using the name Sinbad, one of the* Arabian Nights' *most celebrated travelers. His account was published in 1984 and had a drawing of an Arabian Sinbad with a duffle bag on shoulder heading toward the Statue of Liberty with New York cityscape in the background: the old world meeting the new. The account treats various topics ranging from the history of the American presidency to social issues in today's American society through education and music and ending with a close look at the political career of Thomas Jefferson and Henry Kissinger.*

Washington, DC, obliged me to show her my utmost respect and love because of her romantic atmosphere and her quiet banks on the river Potomac, her clean streets, broad and long, surrounded on both sides by impressive and tall buildings. I have not seen in Washington, DC, the kind of congested crowded streets of other cities—except the other bank of the Potomac which lies in Virginia and Georgetown . . .

As for Boston in Mass. it is really the cradle of American civilization, and the center of revolutionary activities and agitation against the British. Only the one versed in the history of America can appreciate the importance of this city as a capital of art and science since the arrival of the early pilgrims on the Mayflower in the early years of the 17th century. One may say that what is known as New England is the birthplace of American revolutionary figures and American constitution: revolutionary figures such as Washington, Jefferson, Hamilton, and Benjamin Franklin, and Adams . . .

It was natural for me to admire greatly American history which I came to know much later in my life. The reason being that our cultural life in Egypt, after it familiarized itself with Europe did not really know more than the history of France, especially the French Revolution, and less so British history and less so the history of other European countries. For example, we in Egypt are ignorant of the history of modern Germany and know only a smattering of Italian history—jumping from the Renaissance to the modern period . . . I began to read pocket books about American history . . . it is a history of an old European culture making its imprint on a savage landscape, inhabited by the early emigrants and their descendants and managing to turn this new land into a brave new world. Those early emigrants from Europe were indeed civilization-builders who transmitted the civilized habits of their home countries.

The emergence of the USA was truly a momentous event in world history. The challenge for the pioneers was how to cope with a rough environment throughout vast territory that ranges from the Atlantic to the Pacific. The melting of diverse communities of people hailing from different ethnic and cultural backgrounds has created something new, something that blended and modified inherited outlooks, institutions, and ways of life. The American federal system is indeed one of the marvels of human achievements for it blends many diverse elements of good and evil and art and pragmatic spirit and idealism of the English and the Scottish and Irish and the Germanic and the Italian and the Scandinavians and the Checks and the Hungarians and the Spaniards and Jews and Polish and the Russians, . . . etc.

I say it was a marvel, this American experiment in history, for this blend of cultures and communities consecrated religious freedom, racial tolerance, democracy, and equal opportunity for all. The common theme in American life is certainly their intelligence and their experience and their love of freedom and their willingness to protect it and fight for it.

Index

Breinigsville, PA USA
11 March 2011
257420BV00002B/2/P